D0395761

Delivered

Delivered

TRUE STORIES OF MEN AND WOMEN WHO TURNED FROM PORN TO PURITY

Matt Fradd
Editor

San Diego
2013

Delivered
True Stories of Men and Women Who Turned From Porn to Purity
© 2013 Matt Fradd

All rights reserved. Except for quotations, no part of this book may be reproduced or transmitted in any form or by any means, electronic or mechanical, including photocopying, recording, uploading to the Internet, or by any information storage and retrieval system, without written permission from the publisher.

Unless otherwise noted, biblical citations are taken from the
Revised Standard Version of the Bible
(© 1971 by Division of Christian Education of the National Council of the Churches of Christ in the United States of America).

Published by Catholic Answers, Inc.
2020 Gillespie Way
El Cajon, California 92020
1-888-291-8000 orders
619-387-0042 fax
catholic.com
Printed in the United States of America

ISBNs
978-1-938983-46-7 print
978-1-938983-47-4 Kindle, electronic
978-1-938983-48-1 ePub, electronic

All italics added for emphasis in citations from Scripture and ancient texts are the author's.

TOTUS TUUS MARIA

Contents

Foreword

By JASON EVERT

In 2003, while climbing in a slot canyon in southeastern Utah, outdoorsman Aron Ralston dislodged an 800-pound boulder that crushed his right hand against the wall of the canyon. For the next five days, he tried every conceivable method to free his pinned limb, but to no avail. Exhausted and dehydrated—he ended up forty pounds lighter—he began to waver in and out of consciousness, resigning himself to the fact that death was near. He carved his name, date of birth, and presumed date of death into the sandstone wall of the cavern and videotaped a goodbye to his family. Then, he began to hallucinate.

During his vision, he saw a boy, about three years old, walking toward him. Although Ralston wasn't a father, he knew that this child would eventually be his son, and the boy's existence depended upon Ralston's survival. When the premonition vanished, he fashioned a tourniquet. Using the torque of the boulder against his own weight, he snapped his radius and ulna and amputated his arm with a dull pocketknife. After wrapping his arm to control the bleeding, he hobbled out of the cavern into the light, and a rescue helicopter eventually found him.

Aron and his wife, Jessica, were married in 2009, and the following year they welcomed their first child into the world—a boy. The account of his harrowing experience became the 2010 motion picture *127 Hours*.

Despite his life being in jeopardy, Ralston wasn't motivated to act upon the idea of amputating his arm until he realized that the life of his eventual child depended upon his willingness to suffer. It has been said that a knight cannot be brave unless he has love. In the same way, the liberation that Ralston achieved was made possible only through a radical sacrifice ignited by love. He had resigned himself to death. Love alone had the power to set him free.

There are two reasons why I begin a book on pornography with Ralston's story. The first is because I believe that when it comes to the topic of pornography, countless vocations hang in the balance. How many potential marriages have been lost because potential suitors have been too entrenched in laptop fantasies to bother with the demands of commitment and the fears of rejection by a flesh-and-blood female? How many souls have lost sight of their religious vocation because of the spiritual blindness brought on by pornography? How many marriages and families have been decimated? For each of us, the future depends upon our willingness to love.

The second reason I have used the metaphor of *127 Hours* is because many people feel crushed under the weight of their addiction to pornography and have tried countless methods to free themselves, only to find that their efforts are never enough. What they have not realized is that the solution to pornography addiction is love for the porn stars. This might seem counter-intuitive, since we have been taught to shun temptations at all costs. We've been told that erotic images are "bad" and "dirty" and so we must avert our gaze. However, a shame-based approach to overcoming our urges will never stand the test of time. While there's wisdom in having custody of our eyes, something very truthful is missing if the message never goes beyond this.

Since the dawn of creation, the beauty of the human body has been an invitation to love. When Adam and Eve first gazed upon each other's nakedness, they saw their call to love one another through making a total gift of themselves. Nowadays, this divine calling to love too frequently descends to the sterile and thoughtless response of lust.

What are we to do, then, if our desires aren't exactly inclining us toward heaven? First, we must realize that our longings can't be stuffed or ignored. They must be healed. When we fall for the lie that our only two options are repression or indulgence, it's no wonder that so many opt for indulgence. Thankfully, God is calling us beyond both these responses to a love that swallows up shame. For all of us who have been wounded by the effects of pornography, Jesus invites us to bring our ache for union and our desire for what is beautiful to him, patiently allowing him to untangle the distortions in our hearts. Through this painful purification, we gradually become free to love. In his eyes, our desires don't need to be extinguished but set ablaze.

While pornography—and all sin, for that matter—leads to isolation, love draws us toward union. In fact, the virtue of purity draws us to a deeper union with those in the pornographic industry than sin could ever offer. Pure love beckons us to unite ourselves to them through prayer, fasting, and other forms of intercession and activism in order to love them as they may never have been loved before. Their inherent beauty as persons is asking for response in us! Therefore, through the grace of God, every temptation can be transformed into an act of intercession. Each time we resist the allure of a model in an Internet pop-up ad, we ought to turn our hearts immediately to heaven, besieging God with prayers for the person's conversion. By doing this, we're responding to beauty with love.

When we fail to do this, we cave in on ourselves. C.S. Lewis described this well when he discussed the spiritual element of masturbation:

> For me the real evil of masturbation would be that it takes an appetite which, in lawful use, leads the individual out of himself to complete (and correct) his own personality in that of another (and finally in children and even grandchildren) and turns it back: send the man back into the prison of himself, there to keep a harem of imaginary brides. And this harem, once admitted, works against his *ever* getting out and really uniting with a real woman. For the harem is always accessible, always subservient, calls for no sacrifices or adjustments, and can be endowed with erotic and psychological attractions which no real woman can rival. Among those shadowy brides he is always adored, always the perfect lover: no demand is made on his unselfishness, no mortification ever imposed on his vanity. In the end, they become merely the medium through which he increasingly adores himself. . . . After all, almost the *main* work of life is to *come out* of our selves, out of the little, dark prison we are all born in. Masturbation is to be avoided as *all* things are to be avoided which retard this process. The danger is that of coming to *love* the prison.

If you've wavered between loving the prison of lust and longing to be freed from it, you're not alone. The book you're holding contains riveting stories of individuals who have fought the same battle. These testimonies are compelling because none of the individuals seems superhuman in his or her ability to conquer lust. They're genuine. None won an easy battle. All wear the battle scars, and some humbly admit that they still have a long way to go.

While you read these testimonies, I encourage you to look within your own heart to discover why the allure of lust has overcome you at times. Few of us have been immune. While many assume that the magnetism of pornography is triggered simply by lust, I would propose that deeper factors are at play. For many souls, pornography is a false consolation. It's a drug that temporarily numbs unpleasant feelings of loneliness, suffering, anxiety, or boredom. Psychologist Jeffrey Satinover explains:

> The filling of a false need leads to a temporary experience of pleasure which, for a time, overrides the genuine need it is hiding. *But the genuine need is not being met.* After an invariably short time, then, the original distress returns, stronger than ever for having remained wholly unaddressed. The transient experience of pleasure provides but the illusion of fulfillment; the disillusionment only sharpens the true need. Immediately the craving returns, again and again, and soon a habit has been established: the habit of turning to the fulfillment of the false need whenever the true, underlying distress is aroused. And it's always aroused because it's never filled.

Until these deeper needs are recognized and met in a healthy way, the allure of pornography will seem almost irresistible. But if the true needs are fulfilled, porn will lose much of its appeal and fascination.

My prayer for you, as you read this, is that these stories will give you *faith* that God will finish the good work he began in you, *hope* that victory is attainable, and *love* to overcome all temptations.

As you read the following pages, I am certain that the openness and honesty of the contributors will open your own heart and invite you to make an honest inventory of your own life. The authors of this book have made a courageous gift of love to share their stories with the world. Therefore, before you turn this page, would you join me in offering a prayer for them? Let's ask God to continue healing their hearts, minds, and relationships. Let's also pray that God would continue to bless them for their commitment to live out their baptismal promise to reject the glamor of evil and to refuse to be mastered by sin.

Hail Mary, full of grace . . .

Introduction

By MATT FRADD

A little more than two decades ago, it required some effort to seek out and view pornography. One had to drive to the "adult" bookstore or movie theater in the seedy parts of town, or smuggle brown-paper packages from the mailbox and hide them in some secure location until it was safe to view their contents in privacy.

Today, it takes no small effort merely to avoid pornography. Thanks to the Internet, porn can be wherever you are: on your office computer, streamed to your TV at home, even on your phone. Our culture not only makes it easier to access porn, it has casually admitted porn into everyday society. Near-nude bodies and salacious headlines grab our attention from magazine racks at the grocery store; prime time TV shows and commercials are saturated with sexually suggestive images and dialogue.

In every way, pornography has gone mainstream.

It would be sad but not surprising to hear, then, that I caught my first glimpse of soft-core pornography during a visit to a relative's house at the innocent age of eight. I remember being mesmerized and confused, breathless and stunned, paranoid that a grownup might catch me looking at—I didn't know what, exactly—at any moment. I would soon learn that some of my classmates shared a similar fascination, and we began trading lingerie catalogues and creased swimsuit pictures torn from our parents' magazines.

No one ever told me there might be something wrong with pornography. Not my parents, not my priest, not my teachers—no one. And yet, every time I looked at it, I felt ashamed. There seemed to be something not quite right, not quite masculine, about my growing paper harem.

It was not until many years later that I could see with clarity why I had felt shame, why it was so obvious to even my eight-year-old brain that there was something wrong with porn. The reasons are many, and in the stories that make up this book, you will see some of them working their way into—and destroying—the fabric of people's lives.

You will see how porn emasculates men by robbing them of their God-given masculinity and leaving them as mere consumers rather than providers; how it degrades women by reducing the mystery and beauty of femininity to a collection of body parts, making them things to be used rather than persons to be loved; and how it destroys marriages by competing with them, making a mockery of true marital intimacy.

My own path to freedom has been difficult and in many ways is ongoing; but it has been infinitely rewarding. The men and women in these pages likewise serve not just as cautionary cases for the great harm that pornography can do, but as inspiring examples of the even greater work that God performs in the lives of those who seek his help. Porn is more prevalent than ever. But where sin abounds, there grace abounds all the more.

Delivered

From Slavery to Sonship

By JOE McCLANE

There was a man who had two sons; and the younger of them said to his father, "Father, give me the share of property that falls to me." And he divided his living between them.

—LUKE 15:11-12

Like the prodigal son in the Gospel, I took my inheritance from my father in an untimely manner. But it was a spiritual inheritance, and it was passed along unconsciously.

It was 1980, and my father was stationed at Fort Sam Houston in San Antonio when I began to perceive the confusing way he treated my mother. I was six years old. I didn't understand what he was doing, but I knew it wasn't right.

What I didn't know was that my father was addicted to pornography and sexual promiscuity, and he treated my mother like an object instead of a person. Needless to say, this led to divorce, leaving my sister and me hurt and bewildered. All we wanted was our parents together under the same roof, even if they were always at each other's throat.

It was painful to lose my father's presence in my life, and more painful, when I did see him, to witness his new relationships. "Who are all these women?" I thought. "Why are you so familiar with them? They are *not* my mother!"

I found my father's sexual paraphernalia, and at seven, eight, and nine years old I often perused its detailed illustrations. I soon had my own stash of porn. I will never forget when a friend and I were caught with a *Hustler* magazine—in elementary school. My mother busted her butt to provide for my sister and me, and being called to school about this was not the proudest day in her life. She told me it was wrong, but I never heard *why* it was wrong. Sure, it felt dirty, but dirty felt good.

I remember hearing in Sunday school at the Church of Christ that premarital sex was wrong. "Really?" I thought. Even if my instructors tried to answer the question—and I have no doubt that they did—the answer surely didn't take.

It was at this time that my mother's third husband, Wes, entered our lives. Wes was a hardworking man, but he struggled with cocaine, marijuana, alcohol, and—oh yes, porn. By ten years old I had found his stash of pornographic videotapes and began watching them almost daily. Masturbation took root.

My sexual formation was based on my father and stepfather's lifestyle, with its steady stream of pornography. All I ever knew about sexuality, love, romance, the value of women, and relationships was based on what I was watching on TV and finding in the magazines late at night with a flashlight in my bed. I thought this is what "making love" was all about, and what women were good for. This was the inheritance I took from my father at so young an age.

The squandering

Not many days later, the younger son gathered all he had and took his journey into a far country, and there he squandered his property in loose living. And when he had spent everything, a great famine arose in that country, and he began to be in want.

—Luke 15:13-14

As a teenager it was my mission in life to have as many sexual relationships as possible before graduating. I was trying to impress my father; he had countless girlfriends, and so would I. I wanted to show my father that I was becoming a man who was made in his image and likeness, and I desperately wanted him to be proud of me.

So I, too, didn't really consider women as persons; they were commodities to be consumed. They existed to please me, to meet my needs. As a senior in high school I took full advantage of girls who wanted to impress me—you know, to show me they could "meet my needs." They wanted love, affirmation, acceptance, and security, and I wanted their flesh. I convinced one girl to give to me what she should have saved for the man whom God had destined for her in covenantal marriage: her virginity. Not many days later, I was no longer interested in her. Like the images on the porn tapes, she had served my purpose, and I was already looking to my next conquest.

In 1991, the first Gulf War broke out, and I was gung-ho to serve. But because Uncle Sam won't take a seventeen-year-old without a parent's consent, I had to do some convincing to get my mother's permission. I was eager to prove myself to my father. He had served in the Army, and I wanted to serve in the Marine Corps. I'll never forget the day that Sgt. Simmons picked me up at my mother's apartment and shipped me off to boot camp in San Diego.

My father didn't think I had what it took to finish boot camp, so he refused to put the "My son is a U.S. Marine" sticker on his truck until I'd "earned the title." My father loved me, and I think he longed for his son to do better, to be better, than he had, even if he was unable to articulate it. My father went out of his way to show his love for my sister and me, but his concupiscent worldview kept getting in the way.

After three months of blood, sweat, and tears—literally—on my part, my parents looked on in amazement as their remarkably slimmer son, standing tall in his dress blues, received the Marine Corps boot camp's highest award, company honor man. I graduated first out of a class of 450 U.S. Marines. I had earned "the title": I was Lance Cpl. Joseph McClane.

Even though the Marines taught me discipline and some honor, my worldview hadn't changed. In fact, things got worse in the Corps. Drinking, bar fights, strip clubs, porn, and chasing women were pastimes for most of the "Devil Dogs" in my unit. Perverse sexual conquest was all but encouraged by training instructors and senior enlisted folks. Better than winning the lottery, my permanent duty-station orders sent me to Kaneohe Bay, Hawaii. Like a wolf dropped into a pen full of sheep, I was let loose in a paradise full of scantily clad women.

A few summers before, when I lived for three months with my father in Stuttgart, Germany, we shared porn. Although we never spoke about it, I think it bothered him, somehow knowing that this is not what a father is supposed to do.

This kind of sharing developed into an unhealthy mentoring relationship in Hawaii. I was eager to impress my father with tales of all my womanizing. I recall long phone calls and his advice on how to keep one girlfriend from finding out about the other and how to prevent venereal diseases from ruining the party. I earnestly desired to live up to my father's expectations of my sex life and did so to the fullest extent possible.

There was one young girl that stood out. She was eighteen and living with her sister and her sister's husband, who was a staff sergeant attached to my unit. He began inviting me over to his house for dinner and to hang out on the weekends. I began sleeping with his sister-law but, as usual, grew bored pretty quickly. As "luck" would have it, my roommate, Mike, got to know this girl as well, so I broke up with her, giving him a chance to step in—and giving me an easy out.

About a month later she called. "Hey, I'm pregnant," she said, her voice trembling, "and I'm not sure if it's yours or Mike's. I'm scared. I think I want to get an abortion."

"Wow, there is no way I want to be tied down with this chick," I thought. Aloud I responded, "Yes, an abortion—that sounds like a good idea. Do you need money? Tell you what; I'll drive you there."

I checked her into the clinic and waited with her until the nurse called her name. I watched her go around the corner, then left the clinic and walked across the street to a shopping mall where I started scoping out the girls in the food court.

Upon my discharge from the Marines, I returned home to San Antonio and fell into a deep depression. I spent all my time and money on alcohol, strip clubs, and pornography, gaining a lot of weight and wondering about what occupation I should pursue. I ended up at my sister's house in Oklahoma City. There was a radio broadcasting school nearby and she thought it would be perfect for me. I thought, "Yeah, chicks dig a cool deejay. I'll hit it big—a great job, lots of pay, and lots of women."

But ten months later, seven thousand dollars poorer and with a hundred and fifty "no thank-yous" from radio stations across the country, I sold my car so I could buy a train ticket east. My father was living in New Hampshire with his latest girlfriend and I felt that moving in with him would give me a fresh start. It didn't take long to find my father's porn stash and I started using it as often as possible.

I was able to land a couple of radio gigs in southern New Hampshire. One of them was as the news director at an FM station in Nashua. It was a good first radio job, and I had fun as the "sidekick" in the morning drive slot.

It was at my first live remote broadcast, from a Nashua pizza joint in the summer of 1997, that Michelle introduced herself. She had been calling the show, and we had begun to talk off the air as well. I was enjoying our conversations, trying to make myself sound like the "hip" radio guy. She sounded so cute over the phone, but when I saw her I was caught off guard. She was stunning; and I knew right then and there that I wanted to marry her.

I wish I could say that my radio career worked out, but it didn't. I had to make a choice: Follow the radio jobs or follow this woman. By the end of that year I was working for a local telecommunications company, trying to survive on eight bucks an hour. By the time I did get on my knee and present her the ring, I had worked my way up to project manager, which included a decent pay raise. Michelle said yes.

"But if we're going to get married," she said with some hesitancy, "you're going to have to become a Catholic."

I grew up in the Church of Christ, but I had fallen away as a teenager and didn't really care what religion I was. All religions were the same. "Sure, I'll become Catholic," I said.

I signed up for RCIA classes at the cathedral in Manchester. There, I found people who tolerated me and my crazy worldview, foul mouth, and twisted sense of humor without making me feel like the biggest sinner on the planet.

One evening during class, I listened to the facilitator read the Beatitudes in St. Matthew's Gospel and it struck me just how true it rang. "Jesus is talking about seeking holiness," I thought to myself, "and I am everything the opposite of these beatitudes. I mean, I'm not 'free' to live or seek holiness!"

You see, I knew what I would do that night as soon as I got back to the apartment. By then I had high-speed Internet access, and all the porn I could want was a mouse click away.

That was my reality, not seeking holiness. I took every opportunity to indulge in lust—listening to the radio, watching TV, or even just replaying the images in my mind. I was a slave to my passions. But there, in that class, I had a moment of clarity. "It's a good thing I have a long life to live," I thought. "Maybe someday I will be able to seek holiness; maybe someday I will be 'free.'"

The low point

So he went and joined himself to one of the citizens of that country, who sent him into his fields to feed swine. And he would gladly have fed on the pods that the swine ate; and no one gave him anything. — Luke 15:15-16

The priest who gave us instruction tried to set us straight, but I had convinced Michelle that we should live together before marriage. Surely we were living as man and wife, I said—just without all that stuff about commitment of the will, heart, and self that would have gotten in the way of my desire to have my "needs" met.

It was a busy couple of years, completing RCIA, receiving the sacraments, planning the wedding, getting married, buying our first house, and then having Michelle's mother, sister, and two brothers move in months after signing on the dotted line. Yeah . . . good times.

Needless to say, I was feeling overwhelmed and suffocated. My work environment lent itself to my perverse lifestyle, and I was living like a drunken sailor. I yelled at my in-laws constantly, disrespecting them and making them feel unwelcome in my home.

In the spring of 2002, I was laid off. Now, not only was I not bringing home love, charity, and integrity, I was not even bringing home a paycheck. Combine this with the many times my wife had caught me using porn, and she had had enough. She wrote it on a piece of paper: "We're done. I want a divorce."

The turn

But when he came to himself he said, "How many of my father's hired servants have bread enough and to spare, but I perish here with hunger! I will arise and go to my father, and I will say to him, 'Father, I have sinned against heaven and before you; I am no longer worthy to be called your son; treat me as one of your hired servants.'" — LUKE 15:17-19

My world was crashing down around me. I had lost my job; I was losing my house, and now my marriage, too. I had nothing left, nowhere to turn, and nothing to hope for.

Desperate, I turned to the one person I was sure would not be there for me: God. I mean, I was never there for him, so why would he give me the time of day? I took up the Bible I was given in RCIA class and opened it to Matthew's Gospel, chapter five, and began reading those Beatitudes. I didn't know what else to do. I had no idea what to expect, so I just read them over and over again.

The confession

And he arose and came to his father. But while he was yet at a distance, his father saw him and had compassion, and ran and embraced him and kissed him. And the son said to him, "Father, I have sinned against heaven and before you; I am no longer worthy to be called your son." — LUKE 15:20-21

My heart filled with so much emotion and desperation. I got down on my knees and said, "God, I cannot do this. You're going to have to do this." I cannot explain how, but in that instant God allowed me to understand things that I didn't understand the instant before. It was as if scales fell from my eyes. The moment before, I would have rationalized, "We were all born sexual beings. Premarital sex, masturbation, fornication, porn, free love . . . it's all natural, everyone does it. Yes, of course we practice contraception; it's irresponsible not to! I mean, after all, it's her body, and who are you, God, to tell her what to do with it?"

In that miraculous instant, God allowed me great clarity, and I no longer made excuses for my selfish ways. Not knowing exactly how, I understood for the first time in my life that I had to maintain sexual integrity and practice chastity. For the first day since I was about ten years old, I would not masturbate.

The idea that women were not objects to be consumed but were made in the image and likeness of God, to be truly loved and cherished, confused and mystified me. My marriage was permanent, worth saving, worth working for—yes, even worth suffering for—and I would need to beg my wife to stay and work it out.

Another gift I was given that day was an insatiable hunger to know God. In the moment before, I turned to my Bible out of desperation. But now I could not get enough of God's word. I had to have more!

I'd had a personal encounter with the living God, but I had no clue who he was. I was sent on a journey of discovery that would lead me back to the Catholic Church through the graces I had received in the sacraments.

The restoration

But the father said to his servants, "Bring quickly the best robe, and put it on him; and put a ring on his hand, and shoes on his feet; and bring the fatted calf and kill it, and let us eat and make merry; for this my son was dead, and is alive again; he was lost, and is found." And they began to make merry.

—Luke 15:22-24

A few weeks later I entered the confessional, begging God's mercy for decades of debauchery, abortion, and licentious behavior. I didn't really expect to receive it, but, as I knelt at the screen, I heard the voice of Christ through the person of the priest saying the most beautiful words I had ever heard: "I absolve you of your sins."

How many times had I prayed for forgiveness, on my knees even, in the solitude of my bedroom, but had never heard God's voice? Every time I watched porn, masturbated, or had sex with a woman, I was seeking satisfaction, but every time I found only shame. No matter how many times I "confessed" it privately, I never found God's mercy, never received the assurance I so desperately desired.

But there, in that confessional, I came as a slave wallowing in the mud with the pigs, and my Father restored my dignity as a son of the most high God! I was lost but now was found! I was dead but was alive again! God clothed me in his mercy, and I was a slave no longer. Now I am truly free to pursue holiness, to live the Beatitudes. Now I realize that I was not born to lust but to truly love; for Christ came to set us free from sin and death.

Over the next several years our Lord led me to his cross, teaching me the vital tools of virtue, chastity, continence, and objectivity, so that I may combat temptations with a healthy Christian response. I learned to avert my eyes, to cut off the avenues of lust, and to avoid the near occasions of sin, praying to our Lady for help and reminding myself of the dignity and value of women.

I developed the skill to never allow a temptation to enter

my thoughts without a fight. God is truly good. He has blessed me with a beautiful, loving, patient wife and five rambunctious and wonderful children. In spite of my unworthiness, I'm blessed to spend my days sharing the one, holy, catholic, and apostolic Faith with others in my work at Fullness of Truth Catholic Evangelization Ministries. It never ceases to amaze me how God has opened doors; has offered me opportunities to be used by him, for his glory, in the lives of other men who have struggled, and still do struggle, with sexual sin.

Sharing my testimony with others even changed my relationship with my father. Unbeknownst to me at the time, in 2002, the same year God brought me to my knees, my father also had an encounter with Christ and gave his life to Jesus. Given the way he had lived his life, it would take some time before my sister and I realized the fruits of his transformation. I had received many letters over the years from him, but one stands out. He handwrote a letter asking me to forgive him for the sins he committed and for the effects they wrought in my life. He also wrote to my sister and my mother as well as others, asking for their forgiveness. I knew at that point he was no longer the same man. However, it was a talk I gave at a men's conference in July 2008 that changed our relationship. After hearing my testimony, my father wrote me, "It was like getting to know you for the first time, son. . . . I am so proud of you."

The cycle of sin handed on from one generation to the next will end with me. My father inherited pornography addiction and sexual license from his father, as I had from mine. We once talked of conquest together; now, thanks be to God, we talk of what we now love most—Jesus Christ. I have drawn the line in the sand and have declared, "This far and no farther!" My sons will not inherit this from me. They will not find porn in my home. My daughters will know that they are precious in my eyes and daughters of the most high God, never to be used as objects, but to be truly loved and deeply understood. Although my father is not Catholic, we have much in common; and God is leading us on a journey toward the day when we shall sit together at the same table at the wedding feast of the Lamb!

Temptations will come, and I may fall again, but God, in his infinite wisdom, has given us the remedy to the wounds we receive in spiritual combat: the sacraments. What a gift we have in reconciliation—to experience our Father running to meet us on the road, falling upon our neck, and lifting us up from feeding the swine to feasting at his table in his kingdom as his sons!

Don't waste another moment of your life living in your sins, cut off from the life of God. Repent and confess, for, "Just so, I tell you, there is joy before the angels of God over one sinner who repents"! (Luke 15:10).

Freedom and Fullness

By AUDREY ASSAD

As a child, I was prone to shame. The time I rode my bike alone to the corner and back and almost got hit by a car, I cried hard and fast—not because I was scared, but because I was embarrassed. All I could think about was what the driver must be telling his family; maybe that he thought I was stupid for not seeing his car come around the corner; or maybe he was laughing at me because I had cried in front of him. My mother was mystified; I was just plain mortified.

I may have been a little timid, but I could be devious, too. I stepped on my retainer when I was thirteen and I waited a month to tell my mother. When I did, I made up a story about a blind man in the pool. I told her he had kicked me in the face, causing me to bite down hard and break my retainer in half. The poor man had no idea I even existed, a snotty teenager covering her tracks at his expense. Deviousness felt really good for a moment or two, but after a few weeks I was so overcome with guilt that I woke my mom up in the middle of the night in tears and told her what had really happened. Shame had its perfect work that night: It made me tell the truth.

Before I had ever chosen Christ for myself, shame was my fig leaf and, in some respects, the extent of my faith. I can look back at instances in my life and say with certainty that shame was at play in my childish mind, for good or ill, from the very beginning. I made decisions based on it, and I lived in fear of it. It did sometimes cause me to avoid sin, but not for love of God—not at the time.

I was raised in New Jersey in an Evangelical Protestant home (I later converted to Catholicism, but that is a long tale for another time) and was taught to love the word of God and to learn it well. We were educated about the "end times," biblical prophecy, and all the teachings of John Nelson Darby, our denomination's founding father; but one thing I can't remember anyone there teaching about was sex. But even as a child I could deduce from Scripture and my parents' marriage that when two people got married, they "knew" each other in a way that other people didn't know them.

I could tell that there was something physical involved, that sometimes it resulted in babies (I had two younger brothers) and that, as far as I could tell from the little I heard in church, only married people were supposed to do it. Beyond that, I really had no idea what it involved until I hit adolescence and started having crushes on boys. But I couldn't define the new experiences I was having. I overheard comments from adults about modesty, lust, sex, gender, etc., but with little definition or context. And so, I was left to my own devices.

Pornography made its entrance into my life when I was fifteen years old. We lived in a charming little Cape Cod–style house in New Jersey that was cooled by window air-conditioning units, so during the summers the basement was the coolest place in the house. We kept our television down there, along with our computer. One afternoon or evening (I honestly can't remember much about the day) I was down there flipping through TV channels with the remote. As usual, there was a lot of static and fuzz on the higher channels; but as I clicked idly through them, one of the fuzzy screens looked halfway like a decipherable image, so I stopped there, curious.

I cocked my head sideways, squinting. "*What is that?*" I thought. The stripes of static moving up and down the screen only partially disguised bodies that were doing things I had no idea how to contextualize or understand. To this day, the scene brings a flush of mortification to my cheeks, even though it's been more than fourteen years. I suppose I can't get over the fact that I sat down there just staring at those scrambled "adult" channels—and that I kept going back for two years. It is one of my saddest memories.

Although I had precious little understanding of sexuality, I could feel in my bones that something about these strange, fuzzy vignettes was warped. And I felt warped for looking. No one had told me about God's gift of sexuality, but no one had to tell me that this was wrong. But, unlike other times, shame didn't drive me to confess anything to anyone. Until that point, shame had steered me toward the God I feared; but after what I saw, and what that sight stirred inside me, it drove me into a pit of isolation.

From that very first day, the voice of the Enemy condemned me, and I listened. *Dirty*, he said. *You disgusting freak.* Shame was no longer constructive but destructive, and I existed in its iron grip during those dark days and nights. It motivated me no longer to confess but to cover up.

One day, my Sunday school teachers announced that we were going to be starting a series on the harmful effects of pornography. This frightened me and yet relieved me. I was half-convinced my addiction would somehow be discovered by some "anonymous" questionnaire on which my teachers would recognize my handwriting—or perhaps, my discomfort would be visible to them. I'd never been talked to by anybody about pornography before that month-long series. I think part of me believed that at last I would find some freedom, some answers, some remedy to the plague of addiction.

At the series, I was handed a paper that laid out the spectrum of pornography, from "soft-core" to the child and animal-related "perversions." I stared at it blankly, wondering where I measured on the pervert scale. My first encounter with any facts about pornography did little to provide me any hope for freedom, but it sure did reinforce the conclusions of my conscience. This thing was bad—really bad.

I don't remember much else about the study except for a video we watched that revealed that serial killer Ted Bundy was a porn addict. The video listed statistics about serial killers. It said that every serial killer had an addiction to hardcore pornography. Ted Bundy said it himself in an on-camera interview. You can imagine the forest fire of thoughts and questions this ignited within my already reeling mind. I was sufficiently warned about the potential dangers of pornography and too petrified with fear to say anything to anyone, because in my mind all pornography addicts were on their way to being serial killers.

According to the resources we were given, visual pornography (television, computer, magazines, etc.) was a male problem. Women, I was told, sometimes had "struggles" with literature and dime-store novels—the paperbacks in the grocery store with Fabio on the cover embracing a pirate wench or a rich heiress. All those long, flowing tresses and rippling muscles—I had no attraction to those. Even if I had, I would never have dared crack open one of those books in public, much less purchase it and bring it home, so I had no idea what they contained.

I was, however, staying up late at night and sneaking down to the basement to watch the pornography leaking through the channels on our television. So, if only men struggled with visual addiction, was I a freak of nature? Women are sexually objectified in pornography, so did that make me a lesbian? If I even got up the nerve to talk to another woman about this, would she think I was crazy? I was thoroughly confused and convinced myself by the end of the series that I should never say anything to anybody.

Throughout the years of my addiction, I was climbing my way up the ladder of youth leadership at my little church. I was on the board of directors that we set up to help our youth leaders plan events every semester. I helped teach vacation Bible school classes, I sang in the church choir, and I babysat for the weekly Mothers of Preschoolers classes. Limited as my circle of influence may have been, balancing my public reputation with my interior humiliation was a tightrope walk that tortured me day and night. Because I felt no freedom to speak about it, my daily life devolved further and further into a split reality—I had to distance myself from the one thing in order to support the other, on both sides.

I masturbated regularly and hated myself for it. No details are necessary to convey the kind of darkness that hovered over me every night as I fought my own inexplicable urges, wishing that they didn't exist. I didn't understand my problem, but I knew it was wrong, and I felt disgusting. I was afraid to let anyone know for fear of what she would think.

I didn't seek out pornography on the computer. Perhaps I was afraid of seeing those figures too clearly. They were certainly less human on our TV, distorted by static and fuzz. Perhaps it was easier for me to justify watching if I couldn't see their eyes. I hated myself for what I couldn't understand, for what I still didn't really know how to identify. I didn't feel free to talk to my parents or anyone at church about it and definitely not to any of my peers. It wasn't part of our religious culture to open up about such things. But I had been so skittish since my Sunday school pornography lesson that I made a decision: I would stop watching porn—and stop masturbating—on my own. In my mind, it was the only way forward.

So it was then, at seventeen, that I somehow found a way to say no to the nagging cravings. I slipped up regularly, but after about a year, I had managed to stop watching porn. Two years later, at nineteen, I stopped masturbating. Prayer had no significant role in the process, as I was too ashamed to speak to God. Shame, my constant companion in those days, once again drove me to avoid sin; but it also kept me away from the God I longed to know and to be known by.

God wasn't satisfied with that, and neither was I. Life was better without the constant presence of porn, but I was still dying inside. My heart was broken by my own actions. I believed in God, but I didn't know how to let him love me. And I still didn't know how to process the addiction. I didn't understand the core issues behind it. Two years of striving and I had successfully stopped the symptoms, but the illness remained.

I began attending college in South Florida, where I lived with my parents. I commuted to campus and made friends with a small group of students my age who attended a nearby Baptist church. One of them, gregarious and full of zeal, found out that I was a musician and began pleading with me to come and lead worship for their Bible study. Music was only a hobby for me at the time, and I was petrified of singing in front of anybody, but he was persistent. I finally agreed to try it out.

I brought my guitar into the foyer of their youth building

one Tuesday night and tentatively strummed the chords, staring down at the sheet music scattered on the floor around my feet. It was the first time I allowed myself to wonder if maybe I had a role in the church, even with my past. Nobody there was aware of my interior battle, but they welcomed me with open arms. Healing began there, among those ten or twelve college students; singing songs of worship to God, the concept of redemption began forming in my heart.

A friend who attended those Bible studies gave me a copy of *Secrets of the Vine* by Bruce Wilkinson. It sat on my bookshelf for about six months until one night in January 2003, when I was gripped by the urge to open it. I didn't know it then, but it was the spirit of God leading me to its message.

It was just after midnight when I cracked it open. I honestly can't even remember much of what it said, but I sure got the message: Jesus is the vine and we are the branches; and the branches must be pruned—cut—if they want to grow and stay on the vine. I knew in that moment that God was calling me to more than just an iron will against my addiction and a life of shame and isolation. I understood then that freedom meant more than not sinning—it meant receiving the mercy and love of God and finding my identity in that love. My ability to absorb, accept, and truly internalize God's love had been hindered by the same shame instinct that drove me to avoid sin as a child. Now, instead of helping me, it was holding me back. I had to ask forgiveness and then receive it—and move on to better things. Suddenly, I knew and believed that God really did love me; he did actually see something good in me and always had.

I ran downstairs crying like a little girl and practically knocked down my parents' door. I lay down in bed with them and, still crying, told them everything. I'd been silent for four years, and speaking the words aloud for the first time was liberating, frightening, exhilarating. They were forgiving and did not condemn me. I do remember my mom intimating that it was best not to tell other people, but I can't blame her. We were both raised in a culture that made admitting things like that taboo. To this day, I am grateful for her forgiveness and acceptance, as well as my father's. It didn't change how they treated me, and for that I will always be thankful.

I began to pray about whom I should tell, and one by one the Lord brought certain friends to heart. I told each of them—and each of them confessed a similar addiction. I was shocked. One phrase I remember coming from both sides in each one of those conversations was, "I thought I was the only one!" All those years I had thought I was the only one in my prison, but there had been many more behind those same bars. We were just living in isolated cells.

Freedom began to flourish in my heart. Set free from the bondage of the pornography and the shame that had kept me from an abundant spiritual life, I possessed that zeal natural to converts and freed prisoners. It both blessed and frightened others around me, I think.

I had come on staff at that Baptist church as a part-time worship leader involved with the now-burgeoning young adult group. The church had a school attached to it, and once in a while they had me come in and lead worship for a chapel service for the kids—one for the middle-schoolers and one for the high-school students. One morning, I spontaneously told a bunch of yawning, sleepy-eyed high-schoolers about my pornography addiction and my new-found freedom. You'd better believe they sat up straight at that chapel service.

I was overwhelmed by the response of several of the girls, all of whom were in positions of leadership in their youth group. It was my first time telling the story to more than one person, and it made me realize how much freedom there may be for women in bondage to porn, if only those of us who have been delivered would speak up.

As liberating as it was to speak out about my addiction, I was still missing something in my freedom: formation. I was beginning to understand where everything had gone wrong, but I still didn't have a grip on that which was fully and truly right. I could tell groups of people that I had struggled with pornography addiction and that Jesus had rescued me, but that was the extent to which I could explain it. I couldn't talk to teenagers about the real nature of lust, or the horror that is the objectification of human sexuality.

That all changed when I began my exploration of the Catholic Faith at the age of twenty-one, and I met along the way that great work of Pope John Paul II, Theology of the Body (more specifically, Christopher West's lectures on the text). I distinctly remember a line about ghosts and corpses that arrested me: that a corpse was frightening because it was a body without a spirit, and a ghost was frightening because it was a spirit without a body. West said that when you lust after someone, you separate that person's body from his spirit and so you are not giving him the full dignity that a human being deserves.

I was dumbfounded—awed. Someone had finally told me what lust actually was, not just that it was wrong and that I shouldn't do it. All of a sudden it was a lot easier to look temptation in the face and recognize it for exactly what it was: a discontented devil's cheap counterfeit of that which is truly good. Formation gave fullness to my resolve, and I never looked back.

Armed with both freedom and formation, I have begun to share this story more and more often, especially with girls between the ages of thirteen and eighteen. Each time I have done so, my email inbox and Facebook page have been flooded with letters from girls, most of whom say something like, "I thought I was the only one until I heard you say this stuff!"

It would be easy to be discouraged by the number of young women suffering from pornography addiction and by the fact that so many of them are laboring under the illusion that they cannot talk about it without disappointing the people who love them (for that is the Enemy's clever lie). Instead, I have chosen to be a joyful link in the chain of events that will lead many of them to freedom and the knowledge of the merciful love of God. I am truly blessed to participate in interceding for their deliverance. In this way, as in many other ways, God has taken what was broken and disordered and made it new, made it just as it ought to be.

I have been porn-free for twelve years and walking in true freedom from residual shame for nine of those years. For this, and for all things, may all glory be to the Father, to the Son, and to the Holy Spirit—as it was in the beginning, is now, and will be forever. Amen.

The Damage and the Healing

By PETER C. KLEPONIS, PH.D.

My contribution to this book is different from the others. I am not a recovering pornography addict. Nevertheless, as a man, I have been affected by pornography. I am a psychotherapist who has spent much of his career helping men recover from pornography addiction and helping their wives and families who have been affected by it. My personal experience with pornography use, and my experience as a therapist, has helped me understand how powerful a drug it is and how men who are addicted to it truly suffer. In my story, you will learn about why I came to specialize in pornography addiction recovery.

My childhood

I grew up during the 1970s and '80s in a suburb of Philadelphia. My father was an engineer and my mother was a stay-at-home-mom. I am the fourth of five children. My siblings and I attended public schools. Although my family wasn't devoutly Catholic, we did go to Mass on Sundays and attended CCD classes. My family had our share of problems, some serious. Still, we appeared to live a very typical, middle-class suburban lifestyle.

While sex was not considered a dirty thing in our family,

we simply did not talk about it. Still, there was an implied sense of sexual morality in our family. We knew that pornography and sex outside of marriage were wrong. I never got the "birds and the bees" talk from my father, but I received my sex education in public school, which I often refer to as the "basic plumbing course." I did not know if my father or my brothers ever looked at pornography.

I don't remember the first time I viewed pornography, but I know it came from an abandoned quarry near my neighborhood that my friends and I often explored, looking for interesting junk. People would dump trash bags filled with old papers at the quarry. Occasionally, during our junior-high school years, my buddies and I would find pages from old *Playboy*, *Penthouse*, and *Hustler* magazines. I was mesmerized by the pictures of nude women. I would masturbate to those images, which seemed to be burned into my mind. I didn't realize the toxic power of those images. To an adolescent in puberty, they were exciting and pleasurable.

My buddies and I didn't dare take the pictures home, and no matter how we tried to protect them and hide them in the woods, they usually ended up getting wet and falling apart. After talking to hundreds of men about their first experiences with pornography, I found that mine wasn't unusual.

Like many teens, I would feel guilty after looking at pornography or masturbating to it. Pope John Paul II wrote that the opposite of love is use. When I was looking at those images, I wasn't thinking that those women were human beings, children of God, with thoughts and feelings. I didn't wonder about the terrible circumstances that may have led them into the pornography industry. All I knew was the fun and excitement of viewing pornography and masturbation, and I wanted more.

Nevertheless, when I entered high school in the early

1980s, my pornography use decreased. School work, extra-curricular activities, and part-time jobs kept me busy. However, I do remember watching my first pornographic movie during that time. Video cassette recorders had become popular, and a friend who was over eighteen years old rented a pornographic videotape. I was amazed at the graphic, hard-core sex. Although I watched only a handful of porn movies while in high school, they had a tremendous impact on me. If I had had greater access to them, I would have watched more. That was my first taste of how addictive pornography can be for men.

My parents bought a VCR when I was in high school. I remember being excited about renting movies to watch at home. This was before the nationwide video rental chains (and long before automated DVD kiosks and streaming Internet video). Instead, we had a little mom-and-pop video rental store. In the back was the "adult" section, a room where pornographic movies were kept and one had to be eighteen years of age to enter. I would sometimes overhear classmates at school daring each other to sneak in. I have to admit that, out of curiosity, I occasionally snuck into the back room to look at the videos. The packaging alone could have been considered hard-core pornography.

At school, I developed friendships with classmates, both Catholic and Protestant, who were also serious about their Christian faith. We started an after-school Bible study group called "Koinonia." We saw many of our classmates using drugs and alcohol and having sex. We knew we didn't want that lifestyle. Although my new Christian friends helped me avoid pornography, I would still occasionally seek it out, and masturbation was still a problem.

College years

After spending my freshman year of college at an evangelical Protestant school, I transferred to West Chester University, a large Pennsylvania state university. It was a cultural shock. Many of the young men in my dormitory viewed pornography regularly, in magazines and videos. One guy with a large television and VCR in his room ran a porn theater on Friday nights. Even before the Internet, pornography had become a huge part of our culture.

I avoided much of the pornography in college by getting involved in the Newman Association and having a roommate who also stayed away from porn. I was able to surround myself with healthy friends who helped me live a healthy lifestyle. Although I did occasionally slip-up and view pornography, I did my best to stay away from it. Frequent masturbation, however, was still a problem. Unfortunately, I was never taught that it was a sin.

I had always loved helping people, so I started college as a behavioral science major, which involved the study of psychology, sociology, and anthropology. However, it was the 1980s, and, like many of my peers, I aspired to the yuppie goal of wealth, so I changed my major to economics. I graduated from college in 1989 and embarked on a career in financial services.

I moved out of my parents' house and into a house with several devout Catholic men. They also helped me stay away from pornography. It wasn't until the new *Catechism of the Catholic Church* was published in 1994 that I realized that masturbation was a mortal sin. Reading that book helped me truly understand my Catholic Faith. It amazes me that I went through ten years of religious education in my parish and still didn't know my Faith. I thank God that the new *Catechism* was published! Knowing masturbation was a mortal sin, I began working on eliminating it from my life.

Graduate school

I spent most of my childhood and teenage years struggling with depression and anxiety. Unfortunately, this was never detected by my family. For many years, I suffered silently. I knew there was something wrong with me, but I couldn't articulate it. Finally, in 1990, I decided to seek professional help. I found a wonderful Christian therapist who helped me immensely. Through effective counseling and proper medication, I was able to recover.

While I did well in my financial career, I was not happy. The hours were long and the work was boring. In 1993, I realized that if I spent the next forty years sitting in a cubicle crunching numbers I would go crazy. I needed to go back to my first love, helping people. Influenced by my positive experience with counseling, I decided to become a therapist. In 1994, I entered the graduate program in psychology and pastoral counseling at LaSalle University, a Catholic school in Philadelphia.

While the graduate program excelled clinically, it failed religiously and morally. My pastoral counseling classes were taught by an ex-priest who was angry with the Catholic Church and used the classroom as his soapbox. He presented none of the Church's teachings on sexual morality. Later, I realized that I had learned nothing of value in those classes.

My human sexuality classes were no better. They were taught by an ex-Baptist minister who never presented any Catholic teaching on sexuality. We didn't read the *Catechism* or *Humanae Vitae*. In his view, all forms of sexuality— except pedophilia and incest—were valid. He believed that "recreational" use of pornography and masturbation was healthy for men and that viewing pornography together could help a couple's sex life. He even had the class come to his private practice office to watch several hours of pornography, which he called "sexual education films."

By the late 1990s, of course, the Internet had arrived. Luckily, I was spared from being exposed to the pornography that had mushroomed into accessibility at a click of the mouse. I inherited my father's caution with money. Because of the high cost of new technology, I did not purchase my first computer until 2005. Until then, all my Internet use was done at work where it was monitored and pornography was blocked.

While I tried to hold on to my Catholic moral standards in graduate school, I have to admit that, I was influenced by my professors' views. During that time I would occasionally go to video viewing booths at "adult bookstores." It was there that I encountered the true depravity of the pornography industry. The heterosexual videos were often violent toward women; and there were just as many, if not more, gay pornographic videos available. I was propositioned by several men for sex in the booths. Many of them were wearing wedding rings. This is what ultimately turned me off to adult bookstores. I could only imagine the diseases to which these men were subjecting themselves—and their wives.

We never discussed sexual addiction in my graduate human sexuality classes or in my addictions classes. Where I became keenly aware of sexual addiction was in my clinical internship in 1996. I interviewed for positions at several counseling agencies, including Keystone Center Extended Care Unit in Chester, Pennsylvania, a residential treatment center for sexual addiction. It had been founded two years earlier by Dr. Patrick Carnes, the nation's foremost expert in the treatment of sexual addiction. Until then, I had never known that sex or pornography could be addictive. I did not accept the internship because I wanted to work for a Christian counseling agency. However, that interview experience led me to read Dr.

Carnes books on sexual addiction. I accepted an internship with Life Counseling Services, a Christian counseling agency in Paoli, Pennsylvania. It was there that I first encountered and treated clients who were addicted to sex and pornography.

Professional career

I graduated from LaSalle in 1997 and spent the next five years in a variety of positions, gaining professional counseling experience. I worked in a private practice, a public clinic, two colleges, and in corporate training. In 2002, I joined my current practice, Comprehensive Counseling Services in West Conshohocken, Pennsylvania. Although my training is in marriage and family therapy, I decided to specialize in working with men's issues—anger, anxiety, depression, addiction, marital/relationship issues, parenting, career, etc. I wanted to approach them from a Catholic perspective. I also worked with many women, children, and teens struggling with related issues.

It wasn't until I bought my home computer that I discovered all the pornography available online. I was shocked at how widespread and violent it was. By then, I knew it was addictive. I knew I had to stay away from it, especially on the Internet. This was reinforced when I began to treat more and more men who were addicted to pornography.

Some experts refer to Internet pornography as the crack cocaine of porn. I believe this. When I discovered pornography in my early teens, it was photos of nude women in magazines. Today, a young teenager can go online and view—for free—video footage of men violently raping women. The porn that young people are seeing today is far more extreme than the porn I started out with. I believe this leads people to become addicted to it much faster than ever before.

Around 2006, I began to notice a marked change in my clientele. More men were coming to me who were struggling with pornography use. For many, it was their wives who were seeking help. Most of the men were addicted to Internet pornography, and many were acting out because of it. At that point, I knew I had to learn as much as possible about sex and pornography addiction and treatment. I read every book I could find on sexual addiction and addictions in general. I attended conferences on the topic and consulted with other therapists. From my research, training, and clinical experience, I was able to develop an effective treatment program that incorporated Catholic spirituality.

While the next two sections may seem like a departure from my personal story, I feel it is important to discuss the dynamics of addiction and recovery in order to understand the treatment program I developed, which *is* a part of my story.

The path to addiction

Like a coin, all addictions have two sides: emotional and physical.

The emotional side of the addiction is where a man turns to a substance to self-medicate some deep emotional pain. Often, this pain is the result of family-of-origin wounds, such as abuse, addiction, rejection, abandonment, divorce, etc. It can also be caused by deep loneliness, anger, grief, sadness, perfectionism, or insecurity. He is usually unaware of his emotional pain. He discovers a substance that makes him feel really good (i.e., pornography and masturbation). Thus, whenever he is feeling the pain of his emotional wounds, he turns to the substance for comfort. But the comfort is temporary, and he has to return to the substance over and over again to ease the pain. Eventually, he comes to depend on the substance to keep the emotional pain at bay and to function in daily life.

The deep emotional wounds typical in addicts support five core beliefs that feed the addiction:

1. I am unworthy of love.
2. If people really knew me, they would reject me.
3. I cannot count on anyone, even God, to meet my needs.
4. I must find something that I can control that will meet my needs.
5. Pornography/sex meets my needs and is my greatest source of comfort.

The physical side of the addiction occurs when the body develops a tolerance and a dependence on the substance. When a man views an erotic image, chemical reactions occur in the brain. Dopamine production increases and serotonin decreases. This mixes with testosterone and creates a great sense of excitement. Norepinephrine sends a message to the autonomic nervous system to increase heart rate and respiration. A man's heart begins to beat faster and his breathing gets heavier. He may even begin to sweat. A message is then sent down the spinal cord to the genitals for sexual arousal.

Along with all this excitement comes great tension, which must be relieved. This occurs through orgasm, and so the man masturbates. When he orgasms, opiate chemicals called endorphins are released into his brain, creating a sense of euphoria. After the orgasm, there is a great feeling of relaxation. The combination of these sensations—excitement, arousal, tension, orgasm, euphoria, and relaxation—is a powerful drug. The brain craves it and wants to return to it whenever the man experiences any emotional pain or discomfort. This is where the emotional side of the addiction comes into play. It is called creating a neural pathway.

As with any addiction, after a while a tolerance develops. More of the substance is needed to achieve the same effect. Thus, a man will spend more time viewing pornography, and the type of pornography he views will get more extreme: typically more violent, fetishistic, focused on younger subjects, etc. More extreme pornography that may have previously repulsed the man are the very thing he now seeks, because it's the only thing that will arouse him. Many men become unable to perform sexually with their wives. This is because they have become conditioned to be sexually aroused only by pornography.

Thus, a man may initially turn to pornography to ease his deep emotional pain. However, because the effect is only temporary, he needs to return to it over and over again for relief. This is where the emotional side of the addiction develops. Repeated use of pornography allows for the physical side of the addiction to kick in. Ultimately, the man becomes dependent on pornography to function in daily life. If he doesn't get his regular "fix," there can be withdrawal symptoms: depression, anxiety, irritability, headaches, etc. He is fully addicted.

The road to recovery

In recovery, a man will have to go through a detox period where his body becomes used to functioning without the effects of pornography. This is dealing with the physical side of the addiction. He must stop using all porn—cold turkey. It can be a difficult time; however, counseling and support groups are of great help to a man during this period.

Along with the physical detox from porn, the man must work on the emotional side of the addiction by focusing on the corollaries to his unhealthy core beliefs:

1. I am lovable.
2. If people really knew me, they would love me more.
3. I can count on others, including God, to meet my needs.
4. I don't need to find something that I can control to meet my needs.

5. God and healthy relationships meet my needs and are my source of comfort.

This is done by identifying his deep emotional wounds and finding healing for them. Counseling, support groups, spirituality, education, and growth in virtue are needed for this. Helping other men who struggle with addiction is also crucial for recovery. Once his core beliefs are changed to healthy ones, a man no longer needs to use pornography or sex to self-medicate. But because relapse is always a possibility, even after years of sobriety, relapse prevention strategies are developed, and support and accountability to others are always needed. The good news is that a man who is addicted to pornography can find healing and recovery. No one is a lost cause.

A treatment program for Catholics

As I researched recovery programs for sex/pornography addiction, I looked for one that addressed both the emotional and physical sides of addiction. I also wanted one that was distinctly Catholic in its spiritual approach to recovery. There were many successful Protestant and secular programs but no Catholic ones. So, I set out to create one. I studied many programs to see what worked best. There were four elements common to most recovery programs:

1. Complete honesty with self and others
2. The need for support and accountability
3. The need for individual/marital counseling
4. A strong spiritual life

To these elements, I added three additional ones that I have found to be highly effective. I call this a seven-*point* plan for recovery, rather than a seven-step plan, because each point is of equal importance. They are worked on simultaneously. Let me review each point:

1. Self-knowledge and commitment: Here is where a man honestly admits to himself and to at least one other person that he is an addict. There can be no denial in recovery. He must also be fully committed to recovery. If recovery means "moving a mountain," well, by golly, he better be willing to move a mountain!

2. Purifying the environment: In order to overcome pornography addiction, a man must rid himself of all pornography. This includes all magazines, catalogs, DVDs, videotapes, and any porn downloaded from the Internet. It means subscribing to an Internet blocking/accountability service. It can also include major changes to his life. For example, a man who usually passes a porn shop on his way to and from work would need to find a different route. Or, if he has friends who frequent strip clubs, he will need to end those friendships and find healthier ones. Anything that even remotely reminds him of pornography must be removed from his life.

3. Support and accountability: Ask anyone who has been successful in recovery, and he will tell you that he could not have done it alone. One needs support and accountability. This starts by having a group of accountability partners; men who understand the struggle with pornography and are committed to helping each other remain chaste. For men who have an occasional problem with pornography use, their accountability partners can come from a Catholic men's group, such as the King's Men. For those who are addicted to pornography, their

support and accountability must come from a twelve-step group, such as Sexaholics Anonymous (SA) or Sex Addicts Anonymous (SAA). In a twelve-step group, the members help each other recover by working through the twelve steps of Alcoholics Anonymous, modified for sex addiction. Twelve-step groups have been found to be highly successful in helping men in recovery. They are instrumental not only in helping men stay sober but in changing the core beliefs that fuel addiction.

4. Counseling: The first role of the therapist is to help the client identify his triggers for using porn and to develop strategies to effectively deal with or avoid them. This can help the man achieve a healthy level of sobriety. Support groups aid in this task. One often hears of addictions in terms of "self-medicating." It is the pain from deep emotional wounds that men try to medicate with pornography, alcohol, drugs, gambling, food, etc. The therapist helps the man identify the root causes of his emotional pain and resolve them. In healing the deep wounds, the core beliefs that led the man into using pornography can be changed. With the help of the twelve-step group, the counselor can help a man change his core beliefs. Thus, there will no longer be a need to self-medicate with sex, pornography, or any other substance.

5. Spiritual plan: Anyone in successful recovery will tell you he could not have done it without God. One needs to be walking with the Lord daily. As Catholics, we have a wealth of ways to connect with God and receive his healing grace. I recommend daily prayer, Mass (daily if possible), weekly confession, spiritual direction, retreats, and Scripture study. Fellowship with other Catholic

men who understand the struggle is also helpful. Catholic men's groups are invaluable.

6. Education/protecting the family: I have found that a man has to fill his heart and mind with the truth in order to recover from an addiction. I have my clients read books on pornography addiction and recovery and how it affects men, women, wives, children, and teens. This can help increase a man's resolve to recover. I also encourage them to share their knowledge of the danger of pornography with their families and other men.

7. Virtue: One of the best ways to attack any vice is to work on growing in virtue. In my program, I have the men practice virtue daily. This is because virtue permeates all the other points. Virtues such as honesty, courage, humility, chastity, forgiveness, faith, hope, and perseverance are needed in all of the points for healthy recovery. When a man focuses daily on living a virtuous life, it is easier to avoid pornography. This is a uniquely Catholic approach to recovery and is not found in other programs.

Over the past fifteen years, I have worked with hundreds of men and teens addicted to pornography. I have also worked with wives and mothers who have been deeply hurt by this addiction. I have seen marriages and families torn apart and careers lost. However, I have also seen many men in successful recovery. I have seen marriages and families healed and stronger than ever. I know that healing and recovery are possible, and I am passionate about helping those whose lives have been devastated by pornography.

Pornography conferences

In 2009, I was asked to present training conferences to all the priests of the Archdiocese of New York. Priests had approached their diocesan office requesting training. Pornography use was one of the top sins they were hearing in confession. They realized it was no longer sufficient for them to say, "You've made a good confession, stay away from porn, and for your penance say . . ." They wanted to be trained to help men and families affected by pornography.

The conferences were held in June 2010 and were a great success. Other dioceses began requesting similar conferences. From this came the "Fighting Porn in Our Culture . . . and Winning!" training conferences, which have been presented in dioceses across the United States. I have also presented conferences at colleges and seminaries. The need to educate people on how to deal with the pornography plague is immense. People are finally realizing how serious the epidemic is and are ready to address it.

Here and now

Recovery is hard work, and there are falls along the way. However, I have seen many men succeed. I know this is where God has called me to be. When I began practicing psychology fifteen years ago, I never imagined I would be specializing in pornography addiction recovery. But I am convinced that we don't choose our ministries; God gives them to us. We only have to be willing to say "yes" to God. He will take care of the rest.

Some people ask me, "How can you relate to men who are addicted to porn if you are not a recovering addict yourself?" I respond, "Does a doctor have to have cancer to be a cancer specialist?" They usually get it.

I also want people to realize that even those of us in the

fight against pornography are human and struggle at times. As a man, there are many times when I am tempted to view pornography. I am as weak and wounded as anyone. One of the things that keeps me away from pornography is the fact that many people are counting on me to help them in recovery. I could not do my work if I were viewing pornography. I also know how deeply porn hurts wives and marriages. I never want to hurt my wife the way I've seen other wives hurt by porn. In addition, I want to be a good role model for my son. I want him to grow up to be a virtuous, Godly man. To do this I must model it for him.

Words of hope

Pornography addiction is an epidemic in America. Millions of men and teens are enslaved. Wives and families also suffer because of this addiction. Jobs are lost, life savings are spent, and thousands of dollars of credit card debt are amassed. If you or someone you love is struggling with pornography addiction, you know what I'm talking about. I truly do understand your pain.

There is hope! Recovery is possible. No one has to live their life enslaved to this addiction. I urge you to get help. You don't have to do it alone. There are therapists, support groups, and priests available to help you. Don't let fear, guilt, and shame prevent you from getting the help you need and deserve. God wants all men to be strong leaders, providers and protectors of our families, communities, churches, and society. We cannot do this if we are enslaved. God wants you to be free to fulfill the plan he has for your life. I guarantee recovery will be worth the effort.

Beauty for Ashes

By APRIL GARRIS

Growing up, I never knew the love of a father.

My parents split up when I was about six months old and my mother never remarried. I had no contact with my dad until I was six years old, when I started living with him for two months each summer. Flying alone from California to Missouri to visit him was scary and confusing. I still remember the trauma of that first separation, being forced to leave the only parent I knew. My dad was a stranger to me, and I had no idea why I had to leave my home, my friends, and my mommy to visit him.

He was a cold and intimidating man, and I dreaded the visits. I never fit in with anyone in my dad's family, but one uncle was warm and affectionate, and, out of all my relatives, I was the most drawn to him. During my second summer visit, he became my molester. I have blocked most of the incidents from my memory, but it happened several times. I do remember my dad walked in on us—we were in the bathroom, and I was taking a bath—and totally blew up. I don't remember what my uncle was doing. The fact that he paid me so much attention made me feel cared for and I couldn't quite understand that what he was doing was wrong. I never saw my uncle again, and the incident wasn't spoken of. Every time I asked about him, people would change the subject. Now, I am confident that those incidents marked the beginning of my skewed view of sexuality.

At home, I lived alone with my mom. She was a devout woman who loved Jesus but suffered from depression (never diagnosed) and was very moody. We rarely discussed sex. She told me about the basics, but when I had questions about other things (like sexually transmitted diseases and prostitution), she refused to answer them. I had to do my own research and became confused about sex in general. I never saw it as a pure and lovely thing, but rather as something shameful and dirty.

In school, I made good grades but was socially inept. I saw myself as an ugly geek. I had few friends, and I was ridiculed and picked on for most of my school years. I was a loner and isolated myself a lot as I struggled with depression and a poor self-image. I thought few people liked me, and I didn't blame them. I didn't like myself, either. As I grew older, I managed to make more friends but never felt comfortable in my own skin.

I was fourteen when my mom was diagnosed with breast cancer. She was in the hospital for weeks at a time, leaving me alone in the house. I remember one Christmas, when she was in the hospital, decorating the tree and crying over my loneliness. I was too ashamed to open up to anyone about my inner turmoil, so I withdrew. I developed depression and anorexia. At one point, my weight dropped to ninety-nine pounds, and I would black out from not eating. I told myself that I was fat and ugly and needed to lose more weight. The fact that I was in danger of losing the only family member I knew scared me to death, although I never let myself face that fear. I was too distant and numb to reach out to God, although somehow I always knew he was there and, looking back, I know he was protecting me.

Despite all this, I managed to get good grades in school. I graduated from high school early and went to college. Just after my freshman year, I was introduced to speed. I instantly fell in love with it because it gave me a rush of self-confidence, something I had never experienced. It felt good. No longer was I that worthless geek whom people ridiculed. I thought I could do anything. Although I never became physically addicted, there was a powerful psychological draw. There was a huge void inside of me, and the drug helped to fill it and numb my senses. I would continue drugging on and off for most of my life.

During my junior year, I met my husband-to-be. He was my first boyfriend. He was outgoing, funny, and handsome, and we married less than a year later. When he proposed, I said yes, although I wasn't quite sure I was doing the right thing. He seemed like a good catch. I wish I could say that I married him for love, but the truth is, I was deathly afraid of being alone. I figured my mother would be dying soon, and she had always dreamed of seeing me get married. Because of my low self-esteem, I couldn't see anyone else falling in love with me.

A year later, when I was 22, my mother passed away. My husband showed little compassion. During the funeral, when I cried and leaned my face on his shoulder, he didn't respond. He just sat there with his arms crossed. It made me angry and hurt. I spent the night of the funeral consuming massive amounts of speed and sucking up the grief. From that point on, my husband was my only family; I had no one else. I felt I *had* to make my marriage work.

As husband and wife, we never bonded emotionally and romance was nonexistent. We were more like buddies than spouses. There was no affection, no cuddling, and no deep and loving connection between us. I believe we married each other to fill a void; but as the years passed, another void inside me grew deeper. I felt inadequate as a wife. Our sex life was ineffectual and unfulfilling. It was purely physical, with no emotional or romantic element.

A few years into the marriage, I walked in on him in the bathroom as he was looking at porn. I didn't even question him—I immediately walked out and left him alone. When I asked him about it later, he was defensive. I didn't want to start any trouble and figured that my inadequacies were what drove him to look at it. I was hurt, but, as usual, I ignored my feelings. I allowed him to continue looking at it and told myself porn was no big deal.

Eventually, porn made its way into our bedroom and we started using it as a sex aid. I was oblivious to the fact that it was actually destroying the intimacy between us and sex was becoming colder and colder. During our lovemaking, his eyes remained fixed on the TV screen. I told myself that I was being a good wife and helping him. I was in total denial.

Because I did not feel comfortable doing certain things that he was into, the rift between us widened. One day, he suggested that we try "swinging." He said it would be good because he would be able to try out things with other women that I was uncomfortable with, taking the pressure off me. I agreed because I didn't want to deny him what I thought he needed and I didn't want him to become even more dissatisfied sexually.

Swinging was a disaster. Seeing him with other women made me feel more inadequate. So, I made up for it by focusing my attention on other men. I was angry and hoped that he would get jealous. We continued in this lifestyle for a couple of years until I got fed up with the whole scene. We tried to have a normal sex life on our own, but the gulf that had formed between us could never be bridged.

Around this time, a mutual friend, who was a stripper, suggested that I could make a lot of money stripping. Hubby was one hundred percent onboard. I wasn't sure what to think; but by that time I was willing to do anything to keep the marriage peaceable, so I agreed. It was a high-class club in San Francisco. But even so, onstage I felt like a piece of meat. It was a strange experience. I hated the men who came there, yet I wanted them to think I was sexy. I fed off of the attention, but hated what I was doing. I hated how I looked and how I felt, vulnerable and on display. I was exposing myself for guys who didn't care a thing about me.

I remember hubby would come into the club to watch me, and I always hoped that he would see the guys fawning over me. I worked the day shift because it was slower. I couldn't stomach working nights, when the club was packed; all those eyes following me around the club, guys grabbing me, having to make eye and body contact with them. When I got home, my husband always wanted to know how much money I had made. It was never enough. I just wanted him to be proud of me and know that I was desirable. Every day, I dreaded my job. He saw how miserable I was stripping, yet he encouraged me to continue. I lasted only a few months and my husband wasn't happy when I quit. I thought it would be the end of my time in the sex industry. I couldn't have been more wrong.

During those periods when I wasn't sexing for money, I managed to get several jobs, none of them long-term. It seemed that no job I had was good enough for my husband. We were in constant financial trouble, and, with the birth of our daughter, it escalated. We constantly borrowed money from his parents. I felt like a complete loser. One day, the subject of me acting in porn movies came up. He thought it was a great idea and would solve all of our financial troubles. I was sick and tired of being broke and figured that it couldn't be any worse than stripping. I had no idea what I was getting myself into. He took some pictures of me and sent them off to a few agents. A few days later I got a response and headed off to Los Angeles to meet with an agent.

I was completely alone and completely out of my element. My only concern was getting work immediately so that I could make some money and please hubby. I suppose I was also using this to show him how "adequate" I really was. By this time, I was uninhibited and had lost all self-respect. I saw myself as neither valuable nor loveable but as a commodity.

I met with the agent at his filthy apartment. He told me that I could make a lot of money in this business, but first I had to show him how "good" I was. He told me this was standard procedure. I knew nothing about the porn industry but suspected that I was being hustled. At that point, though, I didn't care. I just wanted to come home with a contract. I wadded up whatever self-worth was left in me and threw it out the window. He set up his cheesy video equipment and I did my first "scene" right there in his crappy apartment, with no condom and no protection. It was humiliating and disgusting. After he was done violating me, he made up a bogus contract and sent me home. I never got any work from him.

Instead, my husband became my manager. We moved to Los Angeles and became full-time pornographers. He contacted several porn companies and, over the course of about six months, I made approximately twenty movies. I would do anything that was offered to me. I had no self-respect. We dove headfirst into the lifestyle. I lived my life in a depressed and vacuous daze. On the days when I went to shoot, I tried not to think at all. I would zone out and just go with whatever was happening—and drug out whenever I could.

Being on a porn set was a bizarre experience. The moment you arrive, you get into that "porn mode." This basically means zoning out and transforming yourself into "nympho queen;" ignoring the emotions that are going on inside of you and becoming the person the producer wants you to be. You are a puppet. Filming takes an entire day. After makeup is applied and photographs are taken, the rest of the time you just hang around the set, waiting for your scene to start. While waiting, I would usually go in the back and smoke pot with the other performers. Some of them would be in the bathroom snorting coke. None of us were in our right mind. My husband would always accompany me to the sets, schmoozing with the rest of the "talent" and trying to get more work for me while I was busy having hard-core sex. The pornographers called him my "suitcase pimp."

Filming was a traumatic experience. One fifteen-minute scene can take an hour to shoot. Oftentimes, the performers were rough; and it was never just straight sex—it was a lot of stopping and starting and regrouping and trying to keep up physically, all the while acting like you are enjoying it and wanting more, more, more. The whole experience was mentally and physically draining, and I coped by zoning out. I had sex in a self-induced stupor and the only thought I remember going through my mind was, "This will be over soon. You can do it." I would try to convince myself that I would get used to making porn, or that things would get better. They never did. I had no control over my own body and I was slowly losing my grip on reality. The sheer guilt, along with the emotional and physical exhaustion, drove me even deeper into depression. I didn't even know who I was anymore.

Long days on the porn set left me exhausted and depressed and I had no desire for normal sex with my husband. Even so, I was expected to fulfill my "wifely duties," and seeing me make porn with other men seemed to get him even more aroused. All I was good for was sex and money.

The breaking point came when my husband had scheduled me for a particularly rough scene with two male performers. Days before, I caught an infection and told him that I couldn't go through with the scene. My hope was that he would be sympathetic, cancel the scene, and perhaps show me some kindness. That didn't happen. Instead, he became angry and told me that I was "ruining everything." This scene was going to pay a lot of money. I was going to let that kind of money just slip away? He thought I was an idiot, and I was angered that he had so little concern for my well-being. I was faced with the reality that my own husband cared absolutely nothing about me. I had no reason to justify my behavior any longer and decided that it just wasn't worth it. Shortly thereafter, I quit.

Life after porn was rough. We were still broke, and I had a lot of trouble adjusting to normal life. There were deep emotional wounds, but recovery was impossible. Life was chaotic. I was filled with anger and self-loathing. I sank into a deep depression and started cutting myself. Suicide was not an option for me, so I would take out my anger by self-harming. I loved watching my flesh being cut because it was like revenge against myself. I could not function normally sexually, so hubby would buy me drugs to cope. I was smoking speed and meth, and it exacerbated my mania. One day, he caught me cutting myself and had me institutionalized. I was so exhausted all I did in the ward was sleep and eat. The doctor placed me on lithium. After that, the marriage was pretty much over. Because of my mental state and living situation, he got custody of our daughter. I had lost everything.

By the grace of God, I ended up going back to school and securing a job. I was taken off of medication and things started to look up. Even so, I was lonely. I wasn't looking for a relationship, but I met a man and fell head-over-heels in love. He was handsome, loving, and affectionate. He was also mentally unbalanced and he drank. In my love-induced stupor I overlooked that, and the two of us moved in together. He was unemployed, so I worked and took care of him.

It was an abusive relationship, physically and emotionally. Early on I admitted to him that I had been in porn, and this planted a seed of anger in him that bloomed every time he drank. I was terrified of him in those times. He would kick me, beat me, punch me in the stomach, hold me against the wall by my throat, and say I deserved it because I had been in porn. He called me filthy names, telling me that I was damaged goods and that he was the best thing I would ever have. I believed him. Oftentimes, I would come home from work and he would accuse me of sleeping with the guys on the job because "once a slut, always a slut." When I tried to explain that I hated making porn, he would accuse me of lying. I began to think I was crazy. One time, when he found out that I had been in contact with my ex-husband, he took me to a park and raped me.

He was completely paranoid and would search my phone to make sure that I wasn't calling anyone behind his back. One time, he became so enraged that he sat on top of me and broke my finger. I was terrified to be in the relationship, yet terrified to leave it. I began to hate myself even more for having been in porn. I believed that I deserved the beatings.

This went on for about a year and a half. The breaking point came one morning when he came home drunk after a long night of partying. He was his typical angry self and started ridiculing me for being a "slut," telling me that he knew I loved making porn. Eventually, it became physical. He punched and kicked me. He held me down on the bed and started tearing my mouth open with his fingers. I was bleeding profusely. He held my face in a pillow to suffocate me. He was drunk and crazy, and I was terrified, thinking that he would kill me. I couldn't breathe, and he wouldn't let go. He just kept holding me there.

In desperation, I cried out to the God who had watched over me all of these years. "God," I thought, "if you have any mercy, please send your guardian angels to protect me." At that very moment, my boyfriend let go of my head and went in the other room. I knew that God had saved my life. My boyfriend then ordered me to take a powerful narcotic so that I wouldn't go tell anyone about the beating. I fell into a deep sleep. The next day, I left and never went back. I eventually got a restraining order against him.

I was basically homeless and had no one. I tracked down an old friend, and she invited me to stay with her. She had ready access to drugs, and I consumed mass quantities, trying to forget about my sad life. My life consisted of work, drugs, and partying. I had nothing and no one. God had rescued me from death, yet I was still running from him. After about a year, my friend and I had an argument and she kicked me out.

I lived in my van for about two months while saving up for an apartment. I eventually managed to get off the street and into a place, but I continued drugging and falling deeper into depression. Here I was, thirty-five years old and starting life from scratch. I had lost my family, my home, and all that I had worked for. I felt utterly alone and had all but given up on happiness. Even so, God hadn't given up on me. In his incredible mercy and grace, he looked down upon me and pulled me out of the pit that I had dug for myself. I was an emotional wreck, but God was waiting to piece me back together.

As I drove to and from work each day, I happened upon a Christian radio station. I started listening to the teachings and learning once again about the love and grace of Christ. It was something I had long forgotten about. I knew I could always come back to him, but I didn't realize how much he truly loved me. The messages were like salve to my open wounds, and through those teachings he filled me with the knowledge and understanding of his love, grace, and mercy, which I desperately needed. His word came alive to me, and I came alive as well. He made me realize just how valued and worthy I was. For so long, I believed that I was worthless because I was a throwaway wife who had been in the porn industry. God showed me that I was his beloved child whom he longed to hold again and shower with his love. I was so numb inside, but he taught me how to feel again.

Slowly but surely, he started to rebuild my life. He freed me from the bondage of drug addiction and manic depression and brought me into a fellowship with warm and caring people. For the first time in my life, I had a family. As I started to grow in him and grow deeper into his word, I fell deeper and deeper in love with my Savior. Never in my life had I known such love. It was warm and unconditional.

Next, he put me in contact with Shelley Lubben, another former porn actress. Finally, I had someone to whom I could talk; who understood the kinds of things that I went through in porn; someone nonjudgmental who also loved the Lord. Shortly thereafter, the Pink Cross Foundation was formed and she asked me to be a part of this wonderful ministry that reaches out to women and men in the porn industry to share the love of Christ.

As I look back on everything that has happened, one thing is for certain: Even while I was lost in sin, and even while God was the furthest thing from my mind, through it all, he was protecting me and leading me to that place of repentance and restoration.

I am a new person today. Life can still be hard sometimes, and I still have many things to work out, but having God in my life gives me hope; and I know that he will continue to restore me and help me rebuild, making something beautiful out of my life—beauty for ashes.

To Hell and Back

By MIKE AND ANNE

Anne: Ever since I was a little girl, I was acutely aware that giving your heart to another person could at times bring bliss and euphoria and at other times cause immense pain and disappointment. Time and time again I saw this on TV, in movies, and from watching family and friends. What amazes me is how taken aback I was when I experienced both the highs and lows of love.

I recall clearly how wonderful I felt when I realized I was in love. My first love was Mike. We met in college and quickly grew to enjoy each other's company. We became friends and within two months of meeting began dating. Early on, Mike was brave enough to share with me his struggles with pornography and lust. I remember thinking how fortunate I was to have such an open and honest boyfriend; but I was also scared to hear such things. Could I trust Mike to respect me and not treat me like he did his past girlfriends? Would Mike stop looking at pornography, which I told him was unacceptable if he wanted to date me?

Mike: I grew up in a Catholic home and was blessed to have parents who cared deeply about their faith. In addition to praying as a family on most nights and attending Mass as a family each Sunday, my parents were involved in a community of Catholic families. Dad and Mom went out of their way on Sunday afternoons to drive our family across a large city to attend prayer meetings. My parents sacrificed to send all of my siblings to Catholic grade school and Catholic high school. I was an Eagle Scout, a captain on the football and baseball teams, an avid outdoorsman, and a pretty clean-cut guy. I went to see Pope John Paul II at World Youth Day in Denver, attended a high school retreat at Franciscan University of Steubenville, and went on several mission trips to Mexico.

There was, however, little to no discussion about chastity or God's plan for human sexuality in my home, parish, or Catholic schools. What I learned about sex and relationships came mainly from friends. When I was twelve, a friend from school invited me to his house for the weekend. He said that he wanted to take a shower with me, but I refused. He later showed me his dad's pornographic magazines. I was stunned and captivated by what I saw. We ended up touching each other's genitals for several seconds that weekend, which I spoke to my parents about. But I did not tell them about the pornography.

When I was thirteen, I heard older guys in my Boy Scout troop joking about masturbation, which I soon figured out how to do. For several years, I masturbated on a daily basis. I remember occasionally hearing at my Catholic school that premarital sex and masturbation were wrong, but there was little discussion of why these things were wrong, or how to stop. There was a youth minister who encouraged the boys in my youth group to avoid masturbation and said that accountability with his brother helped him stay free from it as a married man. Other than that, I don't remember another time in my adolescence when I heard a discussion about practical ways to break free from lust.

I attended an all-day sexual purity conference with my youth group and there were stories from older people who had avoided having sex. I thought that chastity was basically not having sexual intercourse. By the end of high school, most of my friends were regularly using pornography, and many had engaged in sexual behavior with their girlfriends. I played several sports in high school, and we sometimes passed around pornographic magazines in the locker room. Time and again, I accumulated stashes of pornographic magazines; but I would throw them away after feeling guilty and tell myself that I would never do it again. My parents gave me no curfews and few boundaries in high school. I can remember only three times that they said anything about sex, and, sadly, I can't say that my parents spent more than two minutes talking to me about sex when I was in high school.

Looking back, there were some pretty strange things that happened in the early years at my Catholic high school. Several times in high school, at a friend's house or on road trips in hotels, several of my classmates and I watched pornographic videos and masturbated in the same room. One day, I was looking at pornography at a friend's house and he informed me that he had read in a porn magazine that if guys engaged in mutual masturbation it was okay and did not mean that they were gay. He was one of the more popular guys in my class who played several sports, and he said that he and another popular classmate had done it. He suggested that we try it and cursed at me when I refused.

There were some drastic changes during my senior year when a priest at our high school taught a course about marriage and chastity. The priest brought in several couples to give testimonies about their marriages. Two of these couples spoke about the importance of natural family planning. I started learning about what love really is and the beauty of God's plan for marriage and sexuality. It was the first theology course that I was really interested in. Looking back, I wish that there had been more discussion about the Church's vision of sex and marriage in my earlier years of high school and even middle school. I am grateful that I received some great information from that priest, and I still have the notes from that class.

In the late 1990s, Anne and I met in college and developed a close friendship before we started dating. Anne was incredibly beautiful, and I was impressed that she played several college sports and did well in her classes. We had the opportunity to study in Rome for a semester, and my prayer life flourished through experiencing the heart of the Catholic Church and walking where martyrs had died for their Faith. Though I struggled with pornography only once during that semester, I knew that I still needed healing. We took a trip to Lourdes and I went into the cold spring water near the cathedral and prayed to be free from pornography and lust. Anne and I were planning to get married within the year and I wanted to be a man of integrity with a great marriage.

Anne: Mike and I were married in June 2001, and, like flipping on a light switch, heart-wrenching pain entered my life. The Internet we had in our home awoke Mike's unquenchable lust from his youth that he had never fully resolved. Why did this happen? How did this happen? Had I done something to bring this on? Was Mike not happy being married to me? We had been married only two months before Mike was hooked. What could I do to stop this? My mother had divorced my stepfather because of his issues with lust and porn.

Pain consumed me. Anger followed—fueled by fear, loneliness, betrayal, confusion, and bitterness. I knew what I could do to stop Mike from looking at porn: I could make him feel the pain that he was making me feel. If he had any clue how devastating this was to me, how hurtful and angry this made me, he would stop. I began to yell, scream, and call him names, desperately trying to let him know how much he was hurting me. My anger contributed to our disconnection, and I soon found that I couldn't make Mike stop, no matter what I tried.

Mike: I bought a pornographic magazine one week before our wedding, thinking that it would be the last time I ever looked at porn. Though I had masturbated to pornography hundreds of times before I had even met Anne, I was convinced that it would all be over after our wedding day. I was not aware about pornography's effect on the brain and the strong neurological and emotional bonds that I had formed with pornography after years of using it.

After our wedding, I struggled with focusing on Anne during times of sexual intimacy. I felt bombarded with the lustful images and fantasies from all of the past pornography. We purchased an Internet connection for our computer early in our marriage, which became a huge problem. I rationalized that at least I wasn't spending any money on Internet porn, although within the first year of marriage I started buying pornographic videos from adult bookstores. I would binge on pornography when I was alone at the house, and I began to look forward to the times that Anne would be away from home. I became isolated from Anne and my friends and family members, and I wondered what people would think of me if they knew how obsessed I was with pornography. After binging on pornography, I would feel terrible. I would go to confession and tell Anne within a few days that I had fallen. But I felt hopeless to break free long-term and knew that it was just a matter of time until I would fall again.

Anne and I conceived our first child during the second year of our marriage. I felt inadequate and scared about being a father. I had access to pornography on a computer at work and I began using pornography more frequently. Pornography is often a gateway for infidelity, and I started looking at dating websites and even posted a personal ad on one of the sites. Anne told me that she would leave if I ever cheated on her, yet I fantasized about how great it would be to be with other people. A few months into the pregnancy, I told Anne that I was thinking about leaving and finding someone else. We ended up losing our son about a week later by miscarriage. I was in a daze at our son's funeral and wondered why I couldn't feel sadness for him. I felt so numb, hollow, and empty. I have faced the fact that the unbearable stress I put Anne through may have caused the miscarriage, and that's not easy to live with.

Things improved with Anne for a while after the miscarriage, but it was hard to feel any hope of long-term victory. We reached out for help with several counselors, but they had little to no experience with pornography addiction. We moved to another state to leave our problems behind, but within several months I was spending lots of time with pornography. I continued going to confession but was ashamed to talk with priests and became frustrated that I was confessing the same sins over and over. There was one priest in particular who was very sincere and recommended some books on chastity. But I was giving up hope that I could ever change.

Anne: I did not know how much more painful it could get. For three years I lived a life of disappointment, confusion, and fear. Each day, I wondered if Mike would tell me he had looked at pornography again. On top of that, it seemed that he needed more and was looking at even more graphic images. Would he cheat? Would he leave me to live the life he seemed to desire? Why did he marry me if this is what he wanted? I felt trapped and miserable and soon fell into despair.

I began to wonder if he would bring a woman to our home while I was at work. I was in my early twenties, and I realized that if Mike cheated on me his behavior could affect my health. I began to fear the possibility of contracting a sexually transmitted disease. This was one of the first revelations that our marriage was not only on the brink of ruin, but that my health and well-being could be in jeopardy.

In January 2004, I gave Mike an ultimatum: Get help or we're done. I was shocked when he chose to seek help and try to salvage our marriage. I had actually hoped that he would just leave so that I didn't have to deal with him anymore; but I was willing to give him a chance so that I knew I had tried everything possible to save our marriage. Mike found a twelve-step group for sexual addiction through the phone book and the group leader told us there was a Christian sexual addiction counseling center in town. He gave Mike a coin commemorating twenty four hours of sobriety; I thought to myself that there was probably a good chance that Mike hadn't been free from pornography for even that long.

Mike: When Anne said that she wanted a divorce, I knew that she was serious. In addition to all of the pornography and dating websites, I had begun to flirt with women at work. Though I had all of these problems in my life, I really did love Anne and did not want to lose her. I also was afraid about what we would say to our family and friends if we divorced. I was not going to give up. I pleaded with her to give me a chance and told her that I would get help, though I did not think there was anyone out there who could help me.

We went for our first session with one of the counselors at the sexual addiction counseling center who had been through recovery himself. The session was humbling for me, but I felt hope for the first time in a long time. The counselor told me that if I was serious about changing, I needed to go to a twelve-step group at least once per week, make a phone call to men in the group every day, read recovery material about sexual addiction each day, and pray at the beginning and end of each day. I was scared before walking into the room for my first Christian recovery group, but I was surprised at how normal and sincere these men were.

Anne and I spent nearly two years in counseling at that center, and I continued going to groups. In the first eighteen months of recovery, I looked at pornography five or six times and was not taking recovery as seriously as I needed to. I found a group that was more committed to recovery and sobriety and began making phone calls and reading recovery material a priority. I developed a close network of friends in the group whom I got to know well. Many of these guys in the group were great Christian men who prayed daily and deeply loved their wives and kids.

The counseling and recovery groups were transformative, and there was a period of nearly five years when I was free from pornography and masturbation. I was able to focus on my studies and finish my undergraduate degree, and I went on to get a master's degree.

Before I found recovery, I had occasionally been free for a few months from pornography, but I can't tell you how amazing it felt to experience years of freedom. We have a merciful God who wants us to have hope and healing. I am grateful for the continued help that I receive from the sacraments, regular meetings with my spiritual director, a weekly twelve-step group, and encouragement from a Catholic men's group, along with daily prayer, phone calls, and recovery material. I still have temptations and struggles with lust at times, but they are much less strong than in the past, and I don't have the feeling anymore that it is hopeless.

Anne: Recovery is not easy. In the beginning, it seemed more difficult than the crisis we had been in for years, since we were used to the cycle of the addiction. This part of our journey took a great deal of work, sacrifice, and time. In our first counseling session, I had been affirmed and empowered for the first time since the addiction began. Mike tried to tell our counselor that his struggles were my fault. Our counselor told him to stop talking and explained to Mike what sexual addiction was and that he was most likely an addict. For the first time, we felt like someone was able to help us.

Our counselor told me that I had done nothing to cause Mike's behavior. He validated me in the decision I had made to not watch porn with Mike or try to be lustful with him, as a previous counselor had suggested I do. These were myths some wives believed would keep their husbands from looking at porn. Mike was addicted to a fantasy world twisted with ideas of what love and sex were. No woman can compete with fantasy. Our counselor was able to share with Mike that in order to stop this behavior he would need recovery groups, marriage counseling, and to begin rebuilding trust and intimacy with me.

Even after finding this incredible help, I was still feeling many terrible emotions. I was still so angry with Mike that even though he wasn't acting out and looking at porn anymore, I felt like screaming at him, and often did. There were times when I didn't think that we would make it. Strangely, I felt resentful towards him and his recovery. Now, he had men in group to talk to, to call and get together and hang out with, while I was at home by myself. Mike was getting better, but I still felt so hurt.

Failure to forgive and trust Mike haunted me. It was difficult for me to even believe that Mike wasn't faking it. I was still expecting for him to walk through the door with his head hanging down and say that he "fell." I had to allow myself to heal and see the changes in Mike's behavior and not just believe his words or promises. These changes included going to a group or two each week, doing recovery reading, making his phone calls, answering his phone when I called, and not blaming me or being mean to me when he was having a stressful day. Mike began to show signs of hope and confidence in himself. For the first time, he was seeing that he could change his behavior and be the man he knew he was called to be. This was promising to me, and I, too, began to have hope in him and us. But what did I have to do to stop being so angry?

Early in our marriage counseling sessions, I resented that our counselor had recommended that I go to a women's support group. Mike's addiction meant I had to go to a stupid group? Wonderful. My poor attitude toward group work caused me to lose years of possible healing. It wasn't until the fall of 2007 that I finally took my own healing seriously. I had believed that once Mike stopped looking at pornography and masturbating, all would be well and our marriage could thrive. After all, that was what had nearly destroyed our marriage in the first place. However, over three painful years Mike had inflicted some deep wounds in me. I had developed my own behaviors to hurt Mike, such as cursing at him, calling him names, and thinking terrible and disrespectful things about him. Mike's acting out with pornography made me feel replaceable, ugly, unwanted, not good enough, and lonely. I had never felt this way before and for years this took its toll on me.

I was finally ready to begin healing those wounds and join a group. Fellowship with other women who could relate to what I had gone through was a huge step in no longer carrying such a burden. I could begin to allow myself to open back up to Mike and to forgive and trust him again. He had been free from pornography and masturbation for several years and I truly believed that our marriage was on the road to redemption. Mike had also discovered Pope John Paul II's beautiful teaching on the Theology of the Body. I still struggled to trust him, especially with anything to do with our faith. I remember thinking, "Who is he to try and tell me what would be good for me and my relationship with God?" Mike was patient, putting to practice what he was learning in his groups and twelve-step work. I finally began to trust him and open my heart to him.

Mike: Our counselors and recovery groups encouraged me to build spiritual and emotional intimacy with Anne on a daily basis through praying together and complimenting her. Our counselor also encouraged us to discuss our emotions on a daily basis, which was an incredible opportunity for me to build more emotional intelligence and maturity. Though Anne did not like the idea at first, we developed a routine of praying together before bedtime and talking about the emotions we had experienced throughout the day. Complimenting Anne each day helped me to cherish the many amazing qualities and gifts that my beautiful wife has.

After a few years of recovery groups and counseling, we attended several Theology of the Body conferences with Christopher West. Before I really dug into the teachings of TOB, I had a hard time with respecting the times of abstinence that Anne and I were going through with natural family planning. I would try to initiate unchaste behavior with Anne. I usually struggled with that at least once a month. I did not want to treat her that way, and I tried just about everything, including accountability with other Catholic men, to help me break free; but the struggles continued.

I read *The Good News about Sex and Marriage* by Christopher West and I was amazed. The level of beauty that Pope John Paul II described with marriage and human sexuality was something I had always been looking for. The concept that loving my wife sexually was meant to be a sign of Christ's love for the Church was completely different than anything I had ever heard. The idea that sexual intercourse was essentially saying our wedding vows through our bodies, and the beautiful vision of our sexual union being an image of the Trinity, were mind-blowing!

I had heard Christopher West present these ideas at his conferences, but carefully reading his book and listening to his Theology of the Body CDs helped this beautiful vision to soak deeply into my heart. Since reading that book in 2007, I have not struggled with lustful behavior towards Anne, and I really haven't felt many temptations to treat her like that anymore. After seeing how amazingly beautiful God's plan for sex and marriage really is, I don't desire to go back to the lustful way I used to treat her. As a man who was deeply addicted to pornography, I may not have been as ready to fully receive the beauty of TOB without the help of recovery groups, sexual addiction books, and counselors. My level of love, passion, and attraction for Anne has never been stronger, and I now see how much I was missing out on before coming across TOB.

Anne: Early in marriage I expected Mike to be my "everything" and for marriage to be the fulfillment of life and living "happily ever after." Not only did we have to deal with the crisis of an addiction, neither of us properly understood what marriage was. I needed not only to learn more about the way God intended marriage, but to build a better relationship with him.

Throughout our entire ordeal, we always went to Mass. We were faithful Catholics who went to confession and regularly received the Eucharist. However, as I learned more about TOB, I discovered that we had barely scratched the surface of our Faith and our vocation of marriage. Mike and I began to thrive, as we were using every tool we could find. We attended marriage counseling, and occasionally we did individual counseling; we were both attending groups and immersing ourselves in the hopeful message of God's vision of sex and marriage through Theology of the Body. Mike and I began to heal, forgive, and raise our hopes to what our marriage could actually become and how it should be lived.

For the first time, I discovered that spouses are meant to help each other get to heaven. Now that we had practical tools, support, trust in each other, and a true vision of sex and marriage from TOB, we began to live our lives better than we had ever envisioned. It seemed as though God used that horrific time in our lives to draw us to him and to learn how to give of ourselves to each other as the gifts God had created us to be to one another. The work we were doing for ourselves and our marriage was paying off. We were rekindling that spark that we once had. We were experiencing the spiritual, physical, intellectual, and emotional intimacy we had learned about in NFP class but had never experienced before. The joy we began feeling for each other, our marriage and our future together was better than any fairytale. I now saw Mike as a precious gift.

As I continued to heal and learn to trust and open my heart to Mike, I knew I needed to turn to God regarding my feelings about starting a family. For years, I feared having children with Mike. But he had made tremendous changes, and although we both knew there would always be temptations, Mike knew what he needed to do to rise above them. He had developed virtues that made him a true man of God. I was ready to truly trust God and Mike, and God was ready to show me that he was listening.

Our most painful moment with Mike's addiction was on April 9, 2003, when I had the miscarriage shortly after Mike said that he was probably going to leave me and find someone else. For six years, I grieved the loss of our little boy. Before we found recovery, I doubted that I could ever trust Mike enough to have children with him. Now that our marriage was thriving, I asked God to speak to my heart about trusting Mike enough to try to have another child. I knew God had heard my heart's desire when Mike and I discovered that we had conceived a baby on April 9, 2009—the six-year anniversary of the miscarriage. He was named after his father so that he would know he has a dad who loves him and wants nothing more than to be the best father for him.

Mike: I now see that God has answered my prayer at Lourdes and has provided much more than hope and healing. We were stunned when we looked at Anne's pregnancy test and thought back to our NFP chart and put the dates together about our son's conception. Though some people might say that conceiving our son on an anniversary of the darkest day of our marriage was just a coincidence, we choose to believe that God is providing even more healing and restoration in our lives. I knew that I needed to name him after me, and I am doing everything I can to leave a legacy to my son and to be a father whom he can look up to.

Anne: Mike and I could not have had the marriage we do now without our long journey through suffering. We gave everything we had to work through it. We battled spiritual warfare—constantly, it seemed—and turned to St. Benedict, St. Michael the Archangel, and our Blessed Virgin Mother Mary, along with our Church's sacraments. God has a weird sense of humor, as he seems to have asked us now to help others with the very problem that nearly destroyed our marriage.

In the beginning of recovery, I imagined that the groups Mike was attending were made up of creepy, perverted men. This is not the case. We have seen that wonderful, normal, good Catholic men, just like Mike, can get caught up in this addiction. What joy we have been able to see in helping couples, through support and recovery groups, find hope and healing from such a devastating addiction. We have seen marriages saved and have received a tremendous amount of grace for our own marriage through these groups. Our troubled times are being redeemed as we continue to work hard on growing in our love for each other. We have found wonderful solace in the Theology of the Body and have made some of the best friends we have ever had since discovering this beautiful work of John Paul II. We are blessed to have the opportunity to share our story and give hope to others who are in similar situations.

Mike: Over the past two years, I became overconfident. I did not attend meetings as frequently and ended up falling back to pornography several times. These struggles have been a sobering reminder that recovery is a lifestyle of being humble, prayerful, and connected with others. I recently attended a men's recovery workshop at a Christian sexual addiction counseling center. The main presenter at the workshop has been free from pornography and masturbation for more than twenty-five years. He still humbly attends twelve-step groups, and he encouraged the men at the workshop to do whatever it takes for their recovery for the rest of their lives, which was inspiring to hear. I have been doing much better with prioritizing my recovery time and prayer, as I did in the early years of recovery, and I feel much more peace, confidence, and joy in my life.

Articles from Jason Evert, Matt Fradd, and ThePornEffect.com have played an important role in my healing. I was shocked by the stories from women who used to be in the pornography industry—of the behind-the-scenes threats, deception, and the sexual abuse of the women involved. I used to think that I was missing out on excitement and fun when I saw the kind of sex people were having in porn videos. But hearing about what happens to these women off camera has helped me to pray for them when I'm tempted by memories from the past.

We have read surveys from several Catholic high schools indicating that nearly half the boys struggle with pornography on a regular basis. Though it is a challenging time with the amount of pornography in our culture, it is also a hopeful time for our Church, with an explosion of new Catholic websites, CDs, and books about chastity, Theology of the Body, and sexual integrity. I have met young men at a local college who formed a chastity group to be accountable to one another and pray together to be free from pornography. Young men at a local youth group have formed a similar chastity group to pray together and be real about their victories and struggles with sexual integrity.

I pray that there will be many more opportunities for Catholics to receive support and healing from pornography through twelve-step programs, counseling, and testimonies. As a father with young children, I want to do everything I can to help my children live with sexual integrity. Even if we do a great job with encouraging them with our story and chastity resources, teens are heavily influenced by their friends in high school and college, and there is much work to do to bring the Church's beautiful vision of sex and marriage into the hearts of the majority of Catholics.

According to Christopher West, more than two-thirds of what the Catholic Church has written about sex and marriage came from Pope John Paul II. I pray that the majority of Catholics will have their hearts filled by the beauty of chastity and Theology of the Body resources and that hundreds of millions of Catholic married couples will experience the tremendous joy and closer intimacy through God's amazing plan for sex and marriage.

Looking back, I thank God that Anne confronted me when she did. I don't even want to think about how bad things would have been without help. I know that I will never be completely free from temptations or lustful thoughts, but building up my "immune system" with these things helps to protect me from the virus of lust. Anne and I are so grateful for the continued hope and healing, and we look forward to more closeness with God and each other. We are so amazed to be parents and we hope that God will bless us with many more children. I know that if God can turn my heart and life around, he can do it for anyone. There is so much hope!

To Worship His Body

By JOSHUA HAWKINS

It has been ten years of sinking into this progression of self-destructive behavior, followed by ten years of trying to stop while sliding farther. I'm only thirty, but I've made thousands of white-knuckled decisions to put down this scourge, only to make about as many decisions to persist in the insanity of this addiction. I know all the reasons it's bad for me—sick, wrong, perverted, demonic, a death-warrant to my career, marriage, children, and life—but something in my heart itches and thirsts for the crack cocaine of lust addicts. Somewhere, in a black chasm of my heart that only Jesus and Satan know, I have a burning desire for a mix of Internet pornography, fantasy, and masturbation.

What I think I'm really looking for is a strange combination of shallow curiosity to escape normal life issues, paired with a deep ache for fulfillment and security. Somehow, over the course of my life, lust became a remedy for a misconnection in my soul I couldn't explain. Now, as a grown man, husband, father, and professional, I know what the misconnection is and to what—or whom—I must be connected in order to live freely. It's a choice I have to make daily: Reach for the light of Jesus, offered to me freely, or recede back into the darkness of my sin. Sometimes I choose wrongly, but Jesus is always waiting to welcome me back. And how happy he is to see me!

I wish this was a story of one, glorious, defining victory over lust; one moment when God rode up on his warhorse, smote my enemies with the fury of his angels, and carried me away from struggle once and for all. I wish I could say, "I was weak, tempted, addicted to porn, but I did A, B, and C, and now I'm strong and it's all easy and I'm cured."

Can Jesus cure me right now? Absolutely. Does he want to? Yes, but in his way, not mine. The truth is, the victory has already been won, but not in this way that my lazy self wishes it to be. Since he entered his final battle on a donkey, not a warhorse, carried a cross instead of a war banner, won the victory through a humiliating death, and later told his apostles that his power is made perfect in weakness—this should indicate just how I will finally reach the glory of the resurrection. I'll win by surrendering to him—not just once, but sometimes hundreds of times a day. And the amazing thing is that it works: I win by surrendering to him, taking up the cross of putting down the lust, and following him. It's not easy, but it is wonderfully simple.

I'm a righteous man who has fallen and is getting up again. Daily, I've had to wearily pick up my shield against temptations and convince my deranged heart that Jesus is the answer, nothing and no one else. If my prayers, fasting, accountability, and reception of the sacraments are not made fully for Jesus, and in openness and reliance on his grace, I will not be able to receive healing.

The problem is not these tools, but rather what lies within me. No reason to give up lust is sufficient in the moment of temptation—not my marriage, children, or reputation.

Though these things so dear to my heart certainly help as reminders to keep fighting, I've found that only reaching to Jesus will offer any hope of victory. I've looked at porn while on the job at a client site, masturbated while viewing porn on a cellphone next to my sleeping wife, and watched porn in my living room while holding my sleeping baby. I don't pretend to be some gloriously horrid sinner—I know I'm capable of much more and, if left to my own devices, will go to any lengths to satisfy this hunger. By God's grace, I'll satisfy it with him alone, through his gifts of my life, marriage, family, and career.

Clearly, for the next two decades, my wife and I will play the greatest part in writing the beginning of our children's life stories and leave them to finish what we've started. I have no desire to blame my parents for my problems; I've made my own choices and must deal with the consequences myself. However, I do need to consider the beginning two-thirds of my life carefully, since it was then that the lust-misconnection ignited and accelerated. I think a perfectionist attitude due to childhood insecurities is one of the taproots of my addiction.

My childhood was wonderful. I grew up in a loving family with parents in a strong marriage. I had all of my material needs met, attended high-end schools, and was at the top of my class in most subjects. I suffered no major traumas and was never abused. So, what went wrong? Why would I reach out to lust? I know it was to fulfill a need—as it still is now—but did I not have everything a child needed? Yes, except in one fundamental area.

My parents were strict and somewhat puritanical. Children were to obey without question, and any deviation was punished immediately and severely. I had an unhealthy fear of my mother, especially when I made a mistake or did something wrong. As a small child, I remember the frequent sting of "punitive discipline," either physically (a spanking) or emotionally (being overpowered by my parents and the feeling of separation that followed).

My parents were not abusive, just strict. I remember a lack of closeness with them, especially when I'd step out of line. My parents acted out of genuine love and concern for me, but my fallen self began to take its identity in my abilities and behavior. Perhaps I was a sensitive child; perhaps most other children would have been fine. But I know that it was here that I began to misunderstand unconditional love. It was here that a fundamental need to know such love was left disconnected.

Even in elementary school I subconsciously felt that love was conditional upon behaving or doing things well, so when I did poorly or misbehaved I felt unworthy of love. My attachment to my parents seemed mainly fear-based, since they ruled with absolute authority. Having a natural predisposition to please people, I didn't react to this environment with rebellious actions, but rather with trying to meet their high expectations and becoming despondent when I didn't.

In school, my academic aptitude earned me a nerd's reputation. This was a new kind of failure: social failure, which I did not know how to study, learn, or plan my way through. I was never badly bullied or ostracized, but the knowledge that some thought of me as lesser in some sense made me want to change that.

In about third grade, kids in school started to joke about masturbation. I had no idea what they were talking about, but I entered into the jokes and the progressively more sex-charged talk. There was this undertone that "everyone was doing it," and merely by talking about it I gained a kind of acceptance. A year or two later, some kids in my neighborhood showed me a pornographic magazine. It was the first porn I'd ever seen, and the image I saw was so explicit that it took me some time to figure out what was going on.

Around this time, I had begun to experience the onset of puberty and was experiencing sexual feelings and changes in my body. A sex education session at school helped me put vocabulary to the feelings, but I felt conflicted as to whether there was something wrong with all of this. I remedied anxious thoughts, an overactive mind, or even loneliness at bedtime by touching myself at night. After experiencing climax for the first time, the hook for using masturbation as a distraction or entertainment became more deeply embedded.

Determined to know the right thing to do, I approached my parents about masturbation. They said it was normal and gave a book called *What Kids Want to Know About Sex*. This added more vocabulary, and I began experimenting more with masturbation. It didn't take long before my friends started trading porn magazines in sixth and seventh grade. I gained a new acceptance at school among the guys. I thought that I'd overcome my sense of isolation. This "success" was a decisive step in relying on lust to deal with my issues when I could not deal with them myself.

I think something deep inside me, something like natural law or my conscience, knew that lust would damage me. C. S. Lewis described masturbation as keeping a harem of shadowy brides that eventually leads a man to fall in love with himself. The women in magazines and posters became the iconic brides of my disordered obsession. From this tender age, I let this shadowy bridal procession into my mind and heart, followed by literally thousands of other women and men to whom I cleaved in a second, then discarded—all to my own satisfaction and in service of myself. I have wept countless times in the arms of my true bride, and she has wept countless times more for me, but my attachment to this massive harem is hard-wired, and only my surrender to God's grace can heal me.

My first two years of high school were spent at a Catholic all-boys school. However, my schoolmates still got the okay in biology class to masturbate as a means of relaxation, whereas there was no formation to the contrary by the Church or other authorities. I let lust sink its roots into me in the form of regular porn and masturbation.

In ninth grade, my family immigrated to the U.S. It was here that I first tried to stop masturbating, and failed. I gained a lot of attention and interest for my foreign accent and was no longer considered a nerd. I was amazed how much the bodies of girls had changed since last I was in a co-ed school two years previously. I reveled in the newfound acceptance, but didn't really know how to interact with a real female. Up to now, my harem arrived when I wanted, did what I wanted, and left when I wanted.

In eleventh grade, I began attending confirmation classes. It was here that I began to acquire a passion for my faith and absorbed all the formation like a thirsty sponge. I wanted to know the truth, especially in matters regarding my sexuality. Finally having a venue to ask questions and do some research, it was confirmed to me that my sexual actions were disordered. I tried harder to stop lusting, and managed to stay away from porn, but I could not do without masturbation.

In twelfth grade, I applied for a position with a missionary organization and thought I'd better make sure I put down this vice before I became a missionary. Though my desire was genuine, I realize now it was a flawed motivation to want to better myself for my own sake or to just be a "good" person. I managed, white-knuckled, to stave off masturbation for most of my senior year and my first mission year, and this inspired some of the guys on my mission team who still struggled with lust—which added to my pride. I thought I'd finally checked it off my self-improvement list and could get on with growing in virtue. I'd left my harem, found Jesus, and been cured from lust—finally!

My first mission year was full of spiritual consolation and excitement. My faith, formation, and zeal grew in leaps and bounds. Though it was genuine growth, I didn't know that my heart was still divided. My entire upbringing of doing things on one's own strength still ran strong in me. Now I risked taking my identity in how my faith had grown, as opposed to how I simply needed to know that I was a son of God. I did not realize how deeply I had let the harem of prostitutes seep into the fabric of my mind and heart. It appeared, at first glance, that I was healed. But when darkness descended again, they would rise again with their ghostly daggers of lust to tear at my soul.

When I went back for my second year, I was appointed as youth minister for a church with many trials and flaws, and this bore heavily upon me when things invariably didn't turn out as I expected. About halfway through the year, under the stresses I'd placed upon myself to succeed in this ministry, I reached for my old drug again. I turned again, regularly, to masturbation to medicate my self-inflicted pain. I had all the spiritual tools a layperson could hope for: daily Mass, rosary, adoration, frequent confession, spiritual direction, brotherhood, and accountability. But somehow I couldn't receive the grace in all this to stave off lust. It was like something was blocked or severed in my heart.

The second mission year ended, stress abated, and my use of masturbation eased. University life presented new stress—secular pressure and far more opportunities to lust. The university student newspaper, bookstores, and poster boards were filled with sex-charged media. Now I was in the realm of people who were "adults" and who could lust unrestrictedly. Despite this, I resisted temptation and tried to hold onto the faith and formation I'd received on my mission years.

My courtship with the woman who is now my wife was tainted with sexual close calls. We remained "technical" virgins, meaning that we did everything else possible except intercourse. Our hearts were definitely not virginal. We both knew it was wrong and would try to avoid these situations, but, alas, our flesh was weak.

Several months before my marriage, I began working the twelve steps with the Serenellian group (named after Allesandro Serenelli, St. Maria Goretti's murderer-turned-convert) and did not masturbate for several months before my wedding. This abstinence continued for a year and a half into the marriage, but lust was merely in hiding during the honeymoon period. I had not surrendered my old ways of perfectionism, negativity, and fear-based thinking and had begun to take hits of lust mentally long before I physically acted on the temptations.

It was crushing for me and my wife to accept I'd masturbated for the first time a year and a half into our marriage. (I always told her when I was having a hard time.) I recall now many times working late at night and wanting to look at porn or masturbate, then going to bed and having the desires evaporate just by being close to my wife—even without sex. But even that honeymoon period would pass. I eventually joined a twelve-step group called Sexaholics Anonymous. I knew that there was nothing lacking in my Catholic Faith and reception of the sacraments, just as there is nothing lacking in Jesus' love. What I lacked was enough faith to grasp the grace and suffer as I let go of the thorn of lust. I lacked the tools to take action on a day-to-day basis.

I finished my undergraduate degree and began working for a legal firm. Any time I was under strain and felt like my life, my work, my household, my wife, or my children were out of my control, I'd start reaching for my drug. I had come to realize that I was trying to control all of these elements in some prideful, perfectionist manner and just couldn't handle it when things didn't turn out my way. To recover from lust, I would have to learn to let go of my other negative attitudes that lust was medicating. I had to treat the disease, not just the symptomatic lust.

I came to realize that total surrender to Jesus can come only in my being fully convinced of the following truth: The more impossible and pathetic my situation, the better a candidate I am to surrender my powerlessness over lust to God. "Rock bottom" with this disease may not be as far away as I like to imagine; however, I have not yet lost my marriage, children, job, freedom, or life. I think I now understand what our Lord meant when he told Paul, "My grace is sufficient for you, for my power is made perfect in weakness" (2 Cor. 12:9).

When I was in Sexaholics Anonymous groups, people talked about an "elite" group of guys who ran a teleconference recovery group that was always successful. They were considered the experts, the "Marines" of lust recovery. Desperate for something—anything—that would work, I was admitted to their ranks. For the first time in years, the downward trajectory of lust turned into an upward flight path of recovery. The rigorous honesty, daily accountability, prayer, and concrete action armed me with the discipline of recovery.

Things went well for about six months until I became weary of the rigidity of the program. I began to go through the motions, do things because I had to, because I'd be accountable to a sponsor at 6 a.m. the next morning, because I was obliged. I did not respond to temptations with the same or greater intensity than the temptation itself. When things got difficult, I was strolling to Jesus when I should have been sprinting.

Not surprisingly, I crashed again. The guys were genuinely surprised. They prescribed a rigorous rerun of my first steps, and again I got up. When I fell again a few months later, I was politely asked to leave the group. I couldn't believe it. I'd been kicked out of a sex addicts group. I was tempted to believe myself a truly hopeless case.

Around this time, my spiritual director pointed me to the writings of St. Therese of Lisieux, which pointed me to a path to which I was previously blind: the way to God's unconditional love. She wrote of being his child—presumptuous, frail, delighted-in by the Father simply because I was his. Made with love, by love, and for love, for it is love alone that counts. Her words breathed into me the message of humble, unshakeable confidence and total abandonment to the Divine Lover.

Here was the key: winning by giving up—turning my back on the war and running to the Savior, and letting myself be loved. To unite both my strengths and weaknesses to him, for without him I could do nothing. Finally, I was connecting to the grace available at every moment to make one a saint.

This had been the crux of every recovery program I had worked: remove the lust, replace it with God's love. Only I was somehow crippled to complete the last part of the equation. Deep in my soul, a place so deep in my childhood that it predated my sexual development and possibly even my memory, the fundamental taproot of my human heart's ability to receive unconditional love had been damaged. I now see this thread of disconnect from unconditional love in my life, a constant need to behave well or regret it, a constant need to perform, to be loved based on what I did. Such an attitude cannot comprehend unconditional love. It was only through the crucible of having my strength crushed and annihilated, such that I had nothing to offer to God except myself, that I could accept his unconditional love.

This was not some rosy romantic notion of love. Reading of the struggles St. Therese faced, and her eventual death, reminded me of a love so strong that it drove God to become man, to be tortured and killed for me. This was a love that would both crown and crucify, and the challenge I face is whether to endure the suffering and martyrdom of giving up the "comforts" of sin for the sometimes bitter chalice of a love that will always satisfy—even through death. There is always that moment when I'm thirsty for the wine of sin and I have to endure the small suffering of refusing it and waiting for my Jesus to quench me with the oceans of his grace. He always does, though there will always be a kind of longing in me during this time of exile.

Oh, and what power this infuses into my wearied pleadings for reprieve from relentless temptation! When the cross of gut-wrenching urges to sin falls once more on my shoulders, as it has thousands of times before, now I'm not running from it. Instead, I receive the cross of temptation willingly—embracing it and doing all things necessary to avoid the occasion of sin and address the temptation—and beg Jesus to save me from sin. In this way, I want only to seek holiness and avoid sin. If Jesus asks me to suffer or endure temptation, I do it by his grace as he did so willingly. I am finally allowing his power to be perfected in my weakness. I'm still just as weak, just as tempted, but now I am uniting myself to him such that it is only his power that saves me.

Ultimately, I will step fully into the victory only when this bodily temple I'm tempted to worship is worn to dust. Until then, my weakness and frailty can be of immense consolation, since I attract Jesus' Divine Mercy all the more. How easily I forget that he's everything I'd ever need, hope for, or imagine! How easily I stray back to the mud puddle of my sin while he patiently points again to the ocean of his love just over the ridge.

I'm sure I will resist, run, and struggle at times, but I do not have to lust any longer if I can let Jesus be the fulfillment for all my empty misconnections. And when I let the Divine Lover in, I find all his treasures are mine. He gives me all things good and holy that only his love can bring. I have finally found what I was looking for. Blessed be God!

Interviews with June

By MATT FRADD

First interview

From 2007 to 2010 my wife, Cameron, and I worked with youths at a small parish in Ireland. It was a blessed time in our marriage as we worked together to lead these teens to the Lord by leading Bible studies, rosary groups, and pilgrimages. A couple of years after we arrived we got word that one of our former teens was working as a stripper in Britain. I got in touch with June (not her real name) while she was still stripping and asked if I could interview her. Here is the first of three interviews we had.

Matt: *June, thanks for agreeing to be interviewed. For the sake of our readers, would you mind introducing yourself a little?*
June: Well, I'm your average young girl. I'm from a small town in Ireland and moved to Scotland to go to university. I love reading and music. I never had many friends growing up and got beaten up a few times whilst I was in school. The other girls in school didn't like me very much, but I just got on with things as usual. I've always been very confident and outgoing, or just really good at faking it.

Would you say you had a typical childhood? How was sex talked about, or not talked about, in your family?
I don't know what a typical childhood is. I guess mine wasn't exactly like nice families you see on TV. My family moved around a lot. My parents were always there but always just a little distant. There wasn't an abundance of hugs and praises in my house, and a lot of things went on between my parents when I was younger that just weren't talked about. But they weren't bad people. There's no sob story. Sex was never talked about in my house. With two Irish-Catholic parents, sex is not something that was ever brought up. I never had "the talk." I think with a lot of Irish-Catholics of their generation it's just the norm not to speak about anything taboo, or any slightly awkward topics.

If someone told you when you were twelve that they thought you'd grow up to be a stripper, what would have been your reaction?
I think if I had been told that, I would have been incredibly upset, but mostly disappointed. I've always been one to have hope for the future. At twelve, I had dreams and aspirations for my future and hoped that I'd be one of the cool kids on campus and maybe have lots of friends and go to parties and be working towards my dream career and finding a nice man. The thought of being a stripper would have taken away all of that hope.

Was there an incident, or multiple incidents, in your adolescence that you think contributed to you choosing the profession of a stripper? Or was it a decision you made out of desperation?
I became sexually active at the age of twelve. I lost my virginity at thirteen. I remember how good it felt to think that a guy wanted me and liked me. All of the girls in my school hated me, so I guess the only people I had left to seek approval from

were the guys. I thought I could make guys like me by getting intimate with them; and if they liked me they wouldn't leave; and if they didn't leave, I wouldn't be alone. I know for sure that I wouldn't have started stripping were it not for the sheer desperation. But I can't lie and say that a part of me hasn't always searched for men's desire.

June, you are currently stripping in Britain. When did you first think of the idea, and why?
Four months ago I was looking for a part-time job in the city I live in and couldn't find one. I had handed my CV [resumé] in everywhere, and nowhere was hiring. I Googled a list of businesses in my area and this strip club was one of them, so I applied. I didn't even really think about it before I did it. It was just kind of on impulse. I needed money because I had run into debt stupidly that my parents couldn't know about, and so I started the job thinking that I'd pay it off quick and then I'd quit.

How did you apply? Was there an auditioning process?
I called up and asked if there were any jobs available and they said, "Yes, will you start tonight?" This was before they'd even looked at me! So I agreed, and I walked to the club from my house later on that night and got a tour of the club and a list of prices for the services the girls were offering.

What was your initial feeling walking into the place? What were the management and staff like?
The boss was friendly enough. The place wasn't as glamorous as I expected it to be. The carpets were dirty, and it was pretty small and smelled awful. As soon as I went into the changing rooms, a few of the older girls came up and started talking to me and giving me advice and being really friendly.

What advice did they give you?
They said things like, "Flirt with the older guys, they have the most money" and "Have a few drinks, you'll need them to loosen up."

What's it like—honestly—stripping in front of strangers who care nothing for you?
It makes me feel sick. A lot of the time I try to imagine they're not there or something, but the biggest part of the job is making them feel special; making them feel like they're unique and that you have a particular interest in them. Looking into their eyes is really important. I hate having to do that because I hate them all. I hate that it's these men who have brought this business into existence. I always have thoughts like, "I hate you so much. Please die. I want to castrate you. Stop looking at me." While I'm in front of them, smiling and staring into their eyes, I feel nothing but loathing.

How much do you usually take home a night?
It varies so much, depending on how busy the club is and how many girls are working. We have to pay £70 commission to the club, and anything we make after that is ours. On average, I got home with about £50. But it could be £10, £20, or £100.

If the advertising is anything to go by, all of the girls are apparently well-rounded nymphomaniacs working at their dream job. How is this true or untrue in your experience?
Me and my close friends in the club are really not nymphomaniacs. We actually talked about this not long ago, and we laughed as we described to each other that we all have the libidos of eighty-year-old women. We want to find nice guys, but not just sex. Some of the older women do talk about

their sexual experiences quite a lot, but they laugh almost too much when they talk about it. It seems like they feel that they have to go along with the cliché of the job.

When's your next "gig"—or whatever you call it?
Saturday. I only work on Saturdays. I'd hate to do it more than once a week. It's mentally and physically exhausting. Having to dance all night is bad enough, but having to sit and flirt with guys and act interested in their lives while they're blatantly ogling and sometimes touching you is the worst part.

Why are you still doing it?
I'm still trying to pay off the £500 debt I'm in without my parents finding out that I'm in debt at all. When I went to university, I wanted to show my parents that I was independent and that I didn't need them and didn't even want any of the approval they never gave me in the first place. I can't face them knowing I screwed up. When I work in the club, I buy so much alcohol to cope with it. Even while I'm getting ready for work, I'll have a bottle of vodka or rum in my room so I can cope with the night, and a lot of money I earn goes on that. But I don't even drink most of the time when I go out with my friends. Just Saturday nights, when I know what I have to face.

Do your friends and family know about you stripping? What are their reactions, and how do you seek to justify to them what you do?
My family does not know at all. They could never ever know. They'd be so angry and embarrassed of me. I wouldn't be shocked if they never spoke to me again if they found out. A few of my friends know I do it. The guys just have a laid back attitude, like, "Well, ya gotta do what ya gotta do," and the girls are just intrigued. One of them even considered applying for a job at the club.

What would you say to a guy reading this who perhaps frequents these strip clubs?

To a guy who regularly goes to strip clubs: You go there to get turned on, or to be made to think that you're special to these girls or that they want you. They don't want you at all. They resent you completely, even if they don't admit it to you or themselves. And I can't understand how a guy could get turned on by the fact that these girls are faking being interested in them. The girls don't want you, they want your money. The girls act like they're having fun, but they're not, because they know you must be pathetic to have to resort to paying for them to pretend they want you. They're the best actresses in the world!

Final thoughts?

The job has made me completely lose faith in love, marriage—yes, nearly all the regulars are married—and decent men. I've come to hate men so much. I've tried having a few relationships since I started this job, and I just couldn't feel anything for anyone anymore. What I'd seen in romantic movies and wished for all my life just doesn't exist. At least not for me.

Second interview

Immediately after our first interview, I asked June if she would consider quitting if she were able to pay off her debt. "Absolutely," she said. I asked if she would be open to my wife and me paying the debt for her, to which she responded, "I'm not that kind of person."

"Let me get this straight," I said. "You're willing to take your clothes off for money, but you're not willing to keep them on for money?"

I think that must have hit home, because after about ten minutes she finally gave in. I told June that while I loved her, I didn't trust her, and I would have to get verbal confirmation from her boss at the strip joint before I could post the check. She agreed. The next day, after speaking with her boss, I mailed June the check, a miraculous medal, and several books that Jason and Crystalina Evert sent me to give to her.

About two weeks later, I contacted her again:

Matt: *Would you mind summing up for our readers what took place after our last interview?*

June: Well, after you and Cam gave me the money to pay off my debt, I called one of my bosses and told them that I quit and I wasn't coming back. He said, "This is very out of the blue. You're a very valuable employee here. We wouldn't like to see you go." And I simply told him that I didn't need to work there anymore and I never wanted to in the first place. That was that! Jason and Crystalina Evert had read my interview and sent me a number of booklets and things to read that really helped me. My faith in love and humanity wasn't instantaneously restored, but the fact that these people I didn't even know reached out to me and tried to help me was overwhelming. What they sent me to read was so touching and full of hope and messages of God's love. I cried my eyes out.

June, I couldn't be happier! How are you coping?

I'm doing well. I love staying in and watching movies on a Saturday night instead of going to work. I shiver every time I walk past the club now. I have started therapy as well to try and overcome my self-hatred, self-harming habits and hatred toward men.

I'm pleased to hear that. What can we, particularly as men, do for women like yourself? Is there any way to reach out to girls stripping and show them they are worth more?

It's tricky. I mean, if I was still working in the club and a man reached out to me and tried to help me, I'd wonder what he wanted in return, and I'd be scared. Don't overdo your compassion for these women and freak them out, but be gentlemen. Treat them with respect. Of course, one practical way of helping them is not to go there!

During your time as a stripper, has any man treated with you with the respect that made you question why you were stripping?
I was hanging out with a popular band not too long ago and we were all drunk in the hotel room after the show. My friend had mentioned to them that I worked at the strip club, and they were all yelling and hollering for me to dance for them. I drunkenly started trying before I eventually stumbled over, and I caught the eye of one of the guys, who walked out of the room. I ran after him and asked him why he walked out and he said, "I didn't like the way they were looking at you like a piece of meat for them to drool over. I didn't want to be a part of that. You're worth more." And that was the most respect I've ever been shown by such a young guy. He told me that I was a princess and that I should quit stripping because I did not deserve to be degraded.

Thank God for men like that, huh? What advice would you give to the ladies out there who may be in hard financial situations and contemplating stripping to make ends meet?
Hmm, that's a tough one. I'm only eighteen; I haven't many ideas on how to make money if you can't find a normal job or someone to help you. But I can say that *anything* is better than getting into that business. It damages women every time they work, and it damages them more than they even realize at the time. Don't sell yourself. If you're struggling, keep trying to find another way to make money, and God will come through for you.

I suppose while we all want a happy ending, the reality is healing is a process, which it sounds like you've begun. Please be assured of our prayers. Thanks again for being so vulnerable and honest.
You're welcome, and thank you.

Third interview

The day I offered to pay June's debt, she had a hard time accepting the fact that Cameron and I didn't want anything in return, so I told her, "Okay, June, here's the deal: We'll pay the debt, if you come over for dinner." She agreed. While she was over, I talked her into going to confession.

Matt: *June, it was so good to see you last week and have you over for dinner. When I asked you that night if you had considered going to confession, your response was, "Absolutely, but I'm terrified!" As nervous as I was about asking you that question, for fear that you'd think I was preaching, I'm glad I did. Would you recount for our readers what was going through your mind when I asked you that question, and why it was something you wanted to do?*
June: Oh, man, my heart started racing just from the mere thought of confessing everything! I felt almost as if I had gone too far now to go and ask for forgiveness. Like I'd done too much damage. I wasn't worth saving. But at the same time, if there was any hope left for me, I wanted to seize it. I didn't want to feel dirty and worthless forever and thought that maybe if I confessed, I could change.

After our conversation I called Fr. James [not his real name] and arranged a time for you to meet him at my house the following week. How were you feeling the day of? Were you tempted to just call me up and make an excuse as to why you couldn't make it?
Oh, yeah. I was so scared and so nervous. I didn't think I'd be able to actually physically speak of all the things I'd done. I

didn't think the words would come out of my mouth. Almost like if I actually came out and spoke the words, it would really have happened. Like everything I'd done was just a bad dream, and if I said them out loud it would all be real. And especially the thought of telling a priest all of it! Oh no—I just hoped maybe he wouldn't show up or that I'd just bolt away running at the last minute.

What were you most afraid of?
I was afraid of having to say the words. I was afraid of fully realizing what I'd done and spilling it all for God to see and judge. I thought my whole world would fall down. I was ready for the Apocalypse!

Lead us through what happened from the time you arrived at our house until Fr. James came to hear your confession.
Well, I got to your house, sat down in your kitchen, and I think my fight-or-flight response kicked in or something, because my heart was pounding and I felt like running right out of that house. I guess you and Cameron could see that I was nervous, because Cameron offered to pray with me before Fr. James came over and you brought the kiddies into another room to play. Cameron prayed for me that I'd sum up the courage to open my heart and confess fully and honestly so that I could be forgiven. I've always been comfortable around Cameron and her big, joyful smile always had this strangely calming effect. It was good to be with her and have her support and encourage me before I had to face all of my sins in front of God.

Tell us your experience of confession.
It was almost surreal. It felt as if everything I was telling Fr. James was being acknowledged somehow but . . . there was no

Apocalypse! After I'd started saying some things and realized that God hadn't darkened the sky and struck me down with lightning, I thought that maybe what I'd done wasn't unforgivable. The more I started talking, the more I realized that there was still hope for me, and although I was happy, it was more of a great revelation, as if all of the time I'd spent thinking and worrying and hating myself for what I'd done wasn't going to last forever. It was a whole new beginning for me.

Final thoughts?
Well, since I've gotten my life back on track and gone through therapy, which has helped a great deal, I'm still in university, studying so that I may help people in the future who have similar issues that I had and unpleasant experiences similar to what I went through. I won't be a hypocrite, pretending I know what they're going through. I'll have firsthand experience of it.

No Greater Love

By JESSICA HARRIS

Some people like to say that they look for love in all the wrong places. For some of us, it is not even about looking in the wrong places; we are looking for the wrong love altogether.

That was the case with me. At the age of seven, I became a victim of divorce. My father had been charged previously with child abuse. Still, I was a daddy's girl, constantly striving for his approval and love. When he left, the entire concept of love became distorted. Love was a fire, and no matter what you did, you would get burned. Better to play the game and get people to like you, but never let anyone close enough to love you.

So began years of anger, rebellion, and searching. My success was wholly dependent on public approval and recognition. I had to be the best, and that was the end of it. If for any reason I did not win, I had failed miserably. Love, in my reality, was not worth my time. Not worth searching for. Not worth the pain of losing.

The day I was introduced to pornography, I was shocked. Sometime before then I had discovered masturbation. I could not even tell you the first time I experimented with it. I had attended public school since the age of eleven, so I was well aware of sex. Many of my classmates had already lost their virginity, and I had considered taking that step to work my way up the popularity ladder. I may have been smart, but I certainly was not pretty. Still, it seemed that only the sexy girls, the cheerleaders and "easy" girls, were accepted. I wanted to be accepted. Pornography, at that point, was far from acceptable, and I certainly had not gone looking for it.

That first taste was repulsive. Research for a school project had gone horribly off course and landed me in a streaming video feed of filth. That first time was much like watching a train wreck. It was so horrible, but at the same time, something drew me in. These women were being accepted. This is what all of those "acceptable" cheerleaders were doing after school in the back seat of the local movie theater. This is what was required of me in order to be accepted. At the time, I wanted nothing to do with it.

While I found the concept of sex intriguing, I really did not enjoy how women were treated in the videos I had found. Something in my gut told me that this was wrong. Though they were being abused and harassed, much like I had been, I was still drawn to it. Those women, even though they were being mistreated, looked happy. They looked like they liked it. I wanted to be happy like them, and I drew the conclusion that true happiness was found in sex.

My family was a strong Christian family. I was raised in the Baptist church, attending service every Sunday and Wednesday. I knew that losing my virginity would have dire consequences with both my family and my church. Most of all, I would lose face and would no longer be the perfect little church girl, and that was important to me. It fed my pride and sense of fulfillment in life. Experimenting with actual sex just did not seem worth the sacrifice.

I set out to find this satisfaction and fulfillment in a different way. I found a free Internet chat room and would wait for "men" to send out messages. I would follow them to a private room and the role play would begin. I would turn to pornography to learn more about what I was supposed to be doing. What did he mean by that? What does that look like? How do you do that? Every day after school I would go into my mom's room, lock the door, put in the headphones and "learn." Then, I would wander into the chat room.

My mom caught me once. With tears running down her face, she asked me what she had done wrong. How had she failed me? What was wrong with me? I promised I would never do it again, but I just figured out how to clear the Internet browser history to keep her from figuring out where I had been.

By the time I graduated from high school, I had left the chat rooms and ventured into the world of hard-core written pornography. On school computers, I would search for "erotica." There were no images involved, and since I was an avid writer in high school, people would see a screen full of text and figure I was simply reading for educational purposes. I spent hours searching for free porn and even attempted to put in fake credit card information a couple of times.

During those years, I began to question my sexuality. Porn was still taboo. I can remember a rare mention of it from the pulpit, but it was always in regards to men. If porn is a male-only thing, I thought, and here I am addicted to it, I must be wired like a man. That means I like women. That means I'm a lesbian.

The search for the "happiness" and acceptance I had seen years before led me down a path that left me less acceptable and more unhappy. Still, I was stuck. I did not want to be there and tried many times to break free. I would save pornographic pictures to a floppy disk (I know, I dated myself there) and then take the disk and destroy it. I would print out pictures and then burn them. I would password-protect the Internet, only to type in the password and gain access again.

It was all a vain attempt to convince myself that I did not need this drug I had stumbled on years before. It was infiltrating my actions and my thoughts. It was ruining my life. I could not have a normal friendship with a guy because I always pictured myself sleeping with him. My spare hours were spent in front of the computer. When I didn't have access to a computer, I would lock myself in my room and fantasize, even getting to the point of writing and illustrating my own erotica. I would destroy it the next day. The high of the moment never made up for the wave of guilt that would wash over me whenever I was finished.

My grades suffered. My family suffered. My life was in shambles. I was stuck, and I knew it. I wanted so desperately to be free, but could not figure out how to get out. I did not know who to ask for help. I feared the judgment of my family, my church, my friends, and God.

My life hit a new low at my high school graduation. The entire time I was addicted to pornography, I was determined to be high school valedictorian. If I make that goal, I thought, I will finally be accepted and be happy. Then, I can leave the pornography behind. I won't need it anymore.

At graduation, I delivered a speech, even including a Bible verse to make my youth pastor and family happy. Yet, when I walked across the stage, the crowd of five hundred was silent. For some, that wouldn't seem a big deal. But for me, that was one of the most defining moments of my life. I had tried everything. I had reached the top, and even the bottom . . . and nobody cared.

For the next month, I sunk low into pornography. It was a drug to ease the pain and the feeling that my life was worthless. I guess it helped me to feel that somebody out there was enjoying themselves and that, somehow, I could have some feeling of enjoyment, even if it was only temporary and was always followed by overwhelming guilt.

Summer left me with hours in front of the computer, alone and unaccountable. In July of that year, I had a drastic encounter with true love and acceptance that can be found only in Christ. Even though I had been raised in the church, I had never dared call into question my personal salvation. My family would disown me. What would they do? What would the church do? I was active in the church. I helped teach vacation Bible school. I helped in the nursery. I sang in the choir. There is no way I could come in front of these people and tell them that all this time I hadn't really believed.

The fear of that judgment was so intense, it crippled me in silence. For me it was worth far more to keep face and keep the acceptance than it was to risk the shame and humiliation of admitting I was a fraud. Then, one night in July, one of my youth leaders admitted that she too, had been living a lie. Her faith had not been real, and she was coming forward that night to confess that and place her faith in Christ.

I figured the youth group would be angry, so I was angry. I felt betrayed by her. I wanted her removed from youth group. How could she stand up there and lead us and not be real? As news of her lack of faith spread, I waited for the judgment that certainly must be coming. That judgment was the reason I refused to even admit that I might not truly know Christ. I waited for it. Waited for her to meet the end that I feared the most.

Instead, she was met with overwhelming joy and acceptance. People came up to her and congratulated her. They were happy for her. They were rejoicing. I sat beside her, completely stunned.

That's it? No condemnation? No reprimanding? No removal from youth group? It was as if God was standing there gently saying, "You've been wrong. This whole time you've been wrong. It's time to stop running." My last excuse wasn't holding water and I was forced to face the reality of my life when compared to the cross of Christ. I struggled long and hard, but that night I came to an understanding and acceptance of the love of Calvary.

I would love to be able to say that the change was instant, but it wasn't. I would love to be able to say that the next morning I woke up and had no recollection of the previous four years of addiction. I can't. The next morning, I still had the same flesh I had the day before. My body still craved that high. I had been in it so long that I felt sometimes I ran on autopilot. My mind would say, "I'm not going to do that today," but my feet would walk into the computer room and I would fall again.

I hit rock bottom in my addiction just a month after coming to Christ. While at a Christian college, I met a guy online. I gave him my information, including my college ID and password, so he could see my picture. Then he asked for pictures of my body, and I obliged. We would stay up until two in the morning, cybering. He would put in special orders for pictures, and I would send them. I was completely ignorant of the fact that I put myself and my roommate in grave danger. This was the next step for me.

When the college deans caught me a month or so later, they reprimanded me for leaving myself logged in on the library computers. "We know this wasn't you. Women just don't have this problem. But if it happens again, we will be forced to send you home." I left at the end of the semester, convinced again that something was gravely wrong with me and ready to just give in and join the porn industry and end the façade.

I attended Bible school the following fall. During an all-girls devotional, the dean of women said, "We know that some of you in this room struggle with masturbation." My breath caught in my throat. It was the first time I had ever heard anyone, especially a Christian woman in a leadership role, verify that women struggled with masturbation and pornography. In that moment, I understood there was hope. Someone knew I was here.

I am sure it is much like feeling trapped in a cave. A friend of mine went spelunking once with some friends, and they became hopelessly lost. When they hadn't returned by sunset, two older women, who had stayed outside the cave, called the park authorities. They were found twelve hours after entering the cave. In those hours, my friend says, they did everything they could to find their way out and then gave up, fearing that they would become further lost. They huddled into a room in the cave and began doing jumping jacks to try and keep their core temperature up. They were literally struggling for survival and were afraid for their lives. Imagine the relief when they heard, "Hello? Is anybody in there?" The irony of it all: they were just yards from the opening.

I felt much like they must have. I wanted so badly to get out of the dark cave of pornography, but I had found myself hopelessly trapped. The more I tried to find my way out, the more lost I became. But now, someone knew I was here, and for the first time ever, I saw a way out.

The dean asked each of us to write our strongholds down on a slip of paper. "A stronghold," she explained, "is any area of your life where the devil is still holding on strong." After we wrote it down, we were to give those slips to two accountability partners. I fought the Spirit as my pen wrote those words: my name and "pornography." There it was, in black and white: I, Jessica, was addicted to pornography, and now I had to tell two people my deepest darkest secret. My flesh was not excited at the prospect and my mind sorted through a variety of different "acceptable" answers: I need to read my Bible more, I need to pray harder; but I knew that if I wanted to get free, this was my only choice. I handed the slips of paper over with tears streaming down my face. I walked back to my room convicted and alone.

Humility. It was the first time I had ever stood up to my pride and faced the fact that the life I had been living was not acceptable. It was the first time I had compared my life to God's standards and realized that I was not a little short. In fact, I was nowhere even close. It was the first step toward freedom.

I would love to tell you that I prayed with my accountability partners and that was it, but that was not the case. In the months following that confession I still battled my lust and the underlying issues of low self-esteem, mistrust, and a twisted view of sex. One of my mentors told me, "You have to love God more than you hate the sin." While that sounded great, I had no clue how to do that. How does loving God look? What does it mean to hate sin? What does it mean to love God more than you hate the sin?

It took a while and a great deal of patience on behalf of my mentors. They constantly listened to my tearful stories of failure and pulled me out of the pit of self-loathing I would throw myself into. I was trying to succeed. I was trying to build up my relationship with God and protect that which he protects. Eventually, I realized that it was probably best for me to build walls tall and then let God shorten them if I had gotten too zealous. I began to protect myself from sex the best I knew how. I asked my roommates to stop talking about it. I stayed away from the young men for a while and did my best to focus on developing my relationship with Christ.

The following summer, I had my first porn-free break. It had been a long journey, and I can remember the joy that came with that. I can do this! My mentors shared in that moment and the moments afterward as I began to understand what I had been missing in all of this: God.

When I had broken floppy discs and burned pictures, God wasn't doing that, I was. When I had reset passwords, that wasn't God. All of those actions stemmed from a hatred of the sin. I hated pornography, I hated the guilt, I hated myself—but I had nothing to replace that hatred. There was no other recourse, no escape but to go back and, essentially, apologize to the pornography for hating it.

With God, for the first time, I understood what it meant to have worth, true worth, not a sexual worth. I realized that my body, with all of its quirks and inconsistences, was fashioned exactly the way he planned. My life was knit together and measured out to fulfill a purpose. I had acceptance because I was accepted into his kingdom. I had love because he had died for me. I had a Father because I had him. All of that truth washed into my life and replaced the years of lies I had believed. Lies about myself, lies about sex, and lies about love.

I wish I could tell you that it doesn't bother me anymore, but over the years I have come to realize that I will always have this weakness. This side of glory there will never be a time when my body completely forgets the thrills it once knew, but that thrill is overpowered by the joy that comes from simply loving God. Now I talk about sex freely, but only in the way God intended. Now I enjoy friendships with Godly young men because I know they are my brothers in Christ. Now I trust people—even love people.

Do I have it all together? No way. There are mornings I wake up and my body wants to relive its glory days. I spend those moments basking in my Savior. In the grace that covers me. In the truth that sets me free. And there, as my desires find their fulfillment in Christ, I find that there is no greater love.

Manly Victory

By MARK HOUCK

Reflecting on my boyhood experience, there is one defining moment when I knew I was being robbed of my innocence: the first time I looked at hard-core pornography.

It was the summer of 1985. I was ten years old, and I was bored. Riding my bike around the streets of Ocean City, New Jersey, I decided to go into a convenience store. As I strolled over to the magazine rack, I noticed one magazine was turned front side down. Curious, I turned it over. As my eyes glanced at the cover, I immediately blushed. My heart started to race, and I looked to see if the cashier was watching me. What I held in my hands was my untimely and impure passage into the world of adulthood, and I knew it.

What I didn't know was that the *Playboy* magazine, which instantly captivated me, was the beginning of sixteen years of indulgence in pornography. "You going to buy that magazine, son?" No, of course not! I turned the magazine over the way I had found it and ran out of the store. As I rode my bike, I couldn't help but think about the images that are burned into my memory to this day. I wanted to go back and see more. The next day, that's just what I did. This phenomenon, I would later discover, is called the "centerfold syndrome," and I was coming down with a bad case of it.

I guess mine is the fairly typical story of a boy discovering the multi-billion-dollar pornography industry. How else does one view their first pornographic magazine unless by happenstance or accident? With the dawn of widespread Internet access about a decade away, most boys my age were stumbling across pornographic magazines or movies either through the negligence of unsuspecting adults or the indiscretion of older siblings and friends. It was the most regrettable event in my young life, although at the time I didn't think so.

In sixth grade, I learned that many of my peers had made similar discoveries. I remember one of my classmates had a porn magazine and introduced me to my first porn video that year. We were alone at his house when this happened. Little did I know it, but the impure curiosity and immaturity of that moment would be something that I would repeat for years as an adult.

The following summer, my father passed away at the age of 43. I was the youngest of four children, and I was traumatized. My dad was buried on my twelfth birthday. For a boy who was just entering puberty and starting to take an interest in girls, it was an injustice of the worst kind. A boy needs his father to answer his questions about his sexuality, and above all, to calm him down about such things as girls or the changes in his body. I was lost. My two older brothers (ages 13 and 17) seemed to have things figured out, so I just followed their example and interests. They both had porn magazines, so I felt justified in looking at them when I found them.

During my high school days, my struggle with pornography was a dark secret. To everyone else, I was a good student and a highly successful athlete. I had a girlfriend. Indeed, on the outside I looked like I had it all together; but on the inside I was struggling, and at the heart of the struggle was my sexual integrity.

I remember feeling lonely during high school. I was confident in athletics, but socially I felt naive. At dances I was awkward and unsure of myself around girls. I was mystified by teammates' talk about things like "hooking up" with girls for sexual encounters. This naiveté only worsened my hunger for pornography. I found myself looking for pornography wherever I could find it. Soft-core pornography, like the *Sports Illustrated* swimsuit edition or my sister's Victoria's Secret catalogue, found its place in my life. Although not as explicit as I wanted, it was close enough. All I wanted to do was quench my impure sexual thirst, and it became a daily routine for me.

Suffice it to say that at the conclusion of my high school days I had a full-blown addiction to pornography and the sin of masturbation. I became so good at compartmentalizing my life that no one would have suspected such a dark secret. All this time I was going to Mass every Sunday and receiving the Eucharist without prior confession—a sacrilege. I guess you could say in some ways I was ignorant of the depth of this sin, but in my heart I knew that it was wrong.

In 1992, I was recruited to play football at the Catholic University of America in Washington, D.C. The fact that it was a Catholic university really didn't mean a lot to me. I made the freshman honor society and earned the starting free safety position on the football team. But my relationship with God and my girlfriend was starting to change.

By the end of my first year in college, my girlfriend from high school and I started to fall into serious sexual sin. Looking back now, I can clearly see how the pornography that had so warped my mind was responsible for introducing these behaviors into what was once a wholesome friendship. Prior to the summer of 1993, I gave away my most precious gift from God: my virginity. Within eighteen months, our sexual sins led us to break up.

I didn't realize it then, but I had become numb to my own sin. I would remain in my numbness for two more years, until one spring day I decided to do something I hadn't done in a long time. In the spirit of the prodigal son (Luke 15:11-32), I decided to return to my heavenly Father. Why, you might ask? What was the reason that I felt so compelled in my heart to submit to God's plan for forgiveness? I guess the answer can be found in my feelings of guilt and shame over my own disgusting behavior and choices.

The night before, I had attended a high school friend's twenty-first birthday party at Georgetown University. This friend was not someone that I was particularly close to, but I had respect for him and looked to him as a model of what I wanted to be, both as an athlete and a student. When I walked into the party, the scene was something straight from the pits of hell. My friend was celebrating with a stripper, no doubt hired by his peer group at Georgetown. Suddenly, I felt like I had in high school—awkward and insecure. I remember there being what seemed like a hundred people crowded into a room at this house in Georgetown. Men and women were cheering my friend on as the stripper teased and taunted him. I remember faking a smile and laughing, so as to break the tension in my heart.

I'm convinced that what happened next was the devil's attempt to humiliate me. My friend told the stripper to grab one of his peers from the crowd and bring him more intimately into the party. The stripper grabbed my hand and proceeded to bring me center stage and mock me in much the same way as she had my friend. I was embarrassed. Looking back now, I feel terrible for that lost soul of a stripper. As I write my testimony, I think of how much I was lost, too.

Afterward, I stopped by the local pub where many Catholic U students went to close out their evenings. I guess I was looking for some comfort or distraction from my own thoughts. As I started to enter the building, a pretty sophomore whom I had noticed that year at the university athletic center came stumbling out the door. You know the guy who embellishes the truth—usually at the high school lunch table—about a girl throwing herself at him? Well, she literally put her arms around me and begged me to take her home.

I had no interest and insisted on going into the bar. But she countered with even more persistence that I take her home. I guess in some ways she spared me the drinking of alcohol, which God knows may have led to any number of other bad choices. I figured, as an act of chivalry, I should escort this young lady home. After all, Brookland (one of the dangerous parts in the District) was no place for a young, attractive woman to be walking home alone—or so I justified in my mind.

I wish I could tell you that I walked her to the door of her dorm and went home, but not so. Although we didn't engage in any sexual sin, I did spend the night in her dormitory. Despite the fact that I had enough integrity not to take advantage of her, I did manage to bring plenty of scandal upon myself, and her, when I departed in the early morning (although the notion of scandal would have been foreign to me).

Looking back now, I can see how my exposure and addiction to pornography allowed those experiences and choices to not only take place, but in a certain sense paved the way for self-deception and rationalization in these moments of temptation. I couldn't bring myself to flee the near occasion sin when I saw it unfolding before me. I was desensitized to the gravity of the moment because I had come to see pornography and my own lustful actions as acceptable and, to a degree, normal for me as a twenty-year-old Catholic Christian man.

So, I guess you could say the reason for me wanting to go to confession the next day was because I finally smelled the stench of my own sinfulness. I was feeling so dirty and brokenhearted over my own impurity and weakness from the night before that I decided I had to do something about it. I hadn't been to confession in four years. Although I was not fully aware of all the sinful baggage I was carrying, I made the best confession that I could, and the knowledge of my actions from the night before was foremost in my mind.

The day I walked into the confessional at the Basilica Shrine of the Immaculate Conception was approximately ten years after my first exposure to hard-core pornography. Walking out of the beautiful Shrine—where Pope Benedict XVI would one day walk and be greeted by so many of my fellow Catholic U alums—was an amazing feeling. I was set free from the sins that were keeping me in chains from the night before. What I didn't know then was that the Lord, through his Holy Spirit, would prompt me to come back hundreds upon hundreds of times before I finally would be able to say that I was free from my pornography addiction and all its secondary effects of masturbation and disordered sexual thoughts and fantasies.

As I reflect back on those days, I am reminded of how gentle and patient God is with each one of his children. He reveals to us only what we can handle at the time. For me, God started my journey by revealing the area that was most keeping me from being in a relationship with him: my lack of sexual integrity.

I wish I could tell you that I walked out of Our Lady's Shrine that day and never looked back. But, as is the case with many of us, we don't always learn the lesson the first time we hear it. It wasn't long before I forgot how offensive my behaviors were to God, and I fell back into my old ways and sinful habits. Sadly, my sins of pornography and masturbation would continue to remain out of control for six more years. And, yes, I would continue in my deadly practice of receiving Communion in a state of mortal sin.

Despite my interior spiritual battle, I managed to graduate college in 1996 with academic all-American honors in football. I was good enough that the New England Patriots sent a scout to watch me practice. On the surface, I had done well. But my life was still a mess, and I was still far from God.

From 1997 to 2000, I spent a good deal of time learning to adapt to life after college, and the depressing realization that I would not play professional football, despite some opportunities to play overseas. It was a difficult transition, and pornography was a dark fixture in my life. I had no real friends to lean on and no understanding of chastity and healthy relationships. Although left to myself much of the time, I did meet and date a couple of women; but neither relationship lasted more than a few months.

Because I was saturated with pornographic images, through the Internet and the purchase of videos, any relationship I did pursue that might have blossomed into something special was quickly dashed as a result of sexual sin. I felt empty inside and in need of much healing and forgiveness. Although I was still attending Mass every Sunday, I was not receiving the grace of the sacraments because I wasn't properly disposed.

In the summer of 2000, I began to volunteer with my parish's youth ministry, and the well-known preacher Fr. John Corapi entered my life. I was twenty-five when I heard him say these words, which are forever burned in my mind: "The blood of your sins is not going to be on my hands on Judgment Day." Fr. Corapi told me that if I continued the way I was going, I was headed to hell.

"No! Not me! But God loves me. I'm a good person, I can't go to hell."

"No," Fr. Corapi said. "Being good is not good enough."

"Where did this doctrine come from?" I thought to myself. Twenty-plus years of Catholic education and never once did I hear anything like this. This chosen instrument of God began to unravel my world as I knew it.

Fr. Corapi revealed to me the deadly nature of my long practice of receiving the Eucharist unworthily. I soon began to understand that I needed to make some serious changes in my life. (As of this writing, Fr. Corapi is no longer serving the Church in active priesthood. Despite his personal vocation crisis, his words are still valid and relevant in my life to this day.)

A short time later, I received my first invitation to reclaim my virginity. I later sealed my commitment to save sex for marriage by signing a purity pledge card in March of 2001 at a Franciscan University youth conference. By making this commitment, I was taking the necessary steps to one day enter into the sacrament of marriage with a whole heart and a pure mind.

I wish I could tell you that this is all it took for the scales to fall from my eyes. I needed to continue to make progress by making better and more generous choices. The first positive choice I made was to commit myself to never receive the Eucharist in an unworthy manner. The next decision I made was to rid myself of all the pornographic triggers in my life—like R-rated and PG-13 movies and magazines like *Maxim* and the *Sports Illustrated* swimsuit edition. I also decided to remove any opportunity to watch television unless I was in the company of others, so as to foster accountability and promote chastity.

As I removed the unchaste materials and the near occasions of sin in my life, slowly I started to experience periods of freedom from lust. I began, also, to see the great benefit of frequent confession and Communion to safeguarding my purity. I felt better about myself. I felt peace knowing that I was in a state of grace and that I was able to hear and feel God's constant presence. I felt an interior joy, the kind of joy that comes from the assurance that God is in charge of my life and that whatever I do and wherever I go, he is with me.

One of my key decisions was to make the time that I fell from grace to the time I received the Lord's forgiveness as short as possible. Later, one brother in the Lord confirmed to me how necessary this step was for him in growing in the virtue of chastity. He said that he strived to make the time between when he fell and sacramental confession as close to zero as possible. In a couple of years, this practice would prove to be essential as the grip of pornography and all its attachments started to loosen its hold on me.

In 2003, the Lord decided that he wanted to take me to another level of intimacy with him. Believe it or not, I was feeling called to speak out on the issue of chastity and saving sex for marriage. I volunteered with pro-chastity groups, such as Generation Life. I was blessed to befriend and be mentored by Molly Kelly, the founder of the chastity movement in the United States. I soon found myself working as a full-time chastity educator.

Even so, I still struggled with impurity. Although in not as disordered and deviant ways as before, I remained very unchaste in my thoughts and actions.

Who would have thought that God would ask me to be the messenger of such an awesome message? I certainly didn't! As I traveled the U.S. and Canada, I took great comfort and strength in the words of St. Francis de Sales: "If you struggle with a virtue, make a public statement about it." His words of wisdom were vital to my progress in purity and the work that I was doing with teens.

By 2006, through God's grace, I was set free from all of my attachments to pornography, both hard- and soft-core. But I continued to struggle with the tenacious sin of masturbation. I may have eliminated the porn in my life, but I was not released from all of the memories and images—that is, until I met my future wife, Ryan-Marie, and made a life-changing decision in my pursuit of virtue and holiness.

It was January 27, 2007, the day I met my Eve. It was at a brisk winter's morning prayer vigil in front of an abortion mill in Philadelphia. I knew I was going to meet her that day, but I didn't know the effect she would have on me. What struck me most were her big, beautiful eyes and eyelashes. After a brief period of awkwardness (not uncommon when you meet the woman of your dreams), I courageously pursued my sister in Christ in a chaste and chivalrous way. I invited her to attend Mass with me following the prayer vigil. Not only was this a great start to our friendship and future relationship, it was the beginning of something that I now claim to be the reason for my complete freedom from the sin of masturbation.

By the time I met Ryan-Marie, I had already gone a significant amount of time without masturbating. I had just experienced two separate stints of approximately ninety days free from self-sex. (Prior to this time, my longest period of freedom was two weeks). I had a deep desire to be set free from this sin prior to entering the sacrament of holy matrimony. I cannot count the number of hours I prayed before the Blessed Sacrament for freedom from this sin. I begged God to grant me the strength to pursue and obtain the virtue of chastity. As much as I had prayed during the previous seven years, the more I often seemed to struggle at times. Still, I continued to press on and pursue the vocation of marriage.

In short order, I discerned that Ryan-Marie was the woman that God had been preparing for me from the beginning of time. I was determined to make myself a sincere gift to her. Following our engagement (only two and a half months after our initial meeting), I made a conscious decision to become a daily communicant. These words from the *Catechism of the Catholic Church* were fresh in my mind:

> Holy Communion separates us from sin. . . . For this reason the Eucharist cannot unite us to Christ without at the same time cleansing us from past sins and preserving us from future sins (CCC 1393).

I knew in my heart that the Eucharist was the only sure way I could become that sincere gift that I longed to be for my future bride. I knew that I needed to stay close to the sacraments of confession and the Eucharist if I was going to have any chance of maintaining my freedom from the sin of masturbation and any future sins against the virtue of chastity.

By the grace of God, it has been seven years since I masturbated. I have been married, as of this writing, just over five years (April 25, 2008). I continue to attend daily Mass as often as I can. I admit it is tougher these days to make daily Mass with our young children's erratic sleep routines. Still, from the days of my son and two daughters' births, I have found three additional reasons to receive the body, blood, soul, and divinity of our Lord and Savior Jesus Christ. I need all the graces I can receive to be the Christ-like example that I am called to be for my four pure gifts from God.

I know beyond any doubt that the graces I receive from daily Mass and frequent confession are the primary reason for my freedom from sexual sin. I believe in my heart that the virtue of chastity can be obtained, and maintained, solely through the grace of God.

For me as a Catholic man, sacramental grace and my vocation as a husband and father are the means by which I am able to stay pure in my thoughts, words, and actions. I believe that true freedom from any habitual sin is possible for anyone, provided he continually avails himself of sanctifying grace through the sacraments of confession and the Eucharist. It is not a magic formula, but it is God's promise to us.

> Ask, and it will be given you; seek, and you will find; knock, and it will be opened to you. For every one who asks receives, and he who seeks finds, and to him who knocks it will be opened. (Matt. 7:7–8)

Thanks be to God!

Epilogue

ARE YOU READY TO BE DELIVERED?

It's my hope that, having read these stories, you will not only be convinced of the destructive nature of pornography, but—if you too are struggling with porn—you'll be motivated to change, grow, and heal. To that end I would like to propose five helpful steps. I call them "steps," but they don't need to be taken in order—they're simply five approaches to healing that are proven to work.

Before we look at these five steps, I think it's important to dispel a myth about purity that many people believe: that it's a *destination*. In reality, purity is not a destination. It is a daily choice. If you are thinking of purity as a state you'll achieve at such and such a time or once you get your prayer life in order, you will almost certainly remain frustrated and discouraged. Why? Because even after we have come to the Lord we are still left with a fallen human nature and "must still combat the movements of concupiscence that never cease leading us into evil" (CCC 978). Sexual purity involves self-mastery, which is a *"long and exacting work* [that] one can never consider . . . acquired once and for all. It presupposes renewed effort at all stages of life" (CCC 2342).

That said, the following steps are crucial and, in my humble opinion, indispensable to anyone who is serious about overcoming his porn problem.

1. Prayer

The importance of prayer may seem so obvious, perhaps even trite, that you might think it isn't worth mentioning. But guess what? When we stop mentioning it, we stop doing it. Many people—perhaps even you— often complain that they just don't have the time to pray, or can just manage to rattle off an Our Father before bedtime.

Lack of time is a lame excuse, because we always find time for *that which we love.*

Despite our busy schedules, we find time for TV, Facebook, waiting in line for coffee . . . and sin. So from now on, don't say, "I don't have time to pray." Be honest and say, "I don't have the love to pray."

And then tell our Lord that. Tell him, "I don't have love," in a similar way to how Mary told Jesus at the wedding of Cana, "They have no wine" (John. 2:3). She didn't make demands of Jesus, she simply stated a fact, trusting that he would act. We should do likewise.

Allow me to suggest three methods of prayer that have been of great help to me, followed by two short prayers for purity of heart when in a moment of temptation to lust.

The Rosary

"To recite the Rosary," wrote Pope John Paul II, "is nothing other than to contemplate with Mary the face of Christ." To commit to praying the rosary, perhaps even daily, is to commit to spending fifteen to twenty minutes in quiet contemplation. Often those who habitually use pornography say they experience an inner disquiet that can make contemplation seem almost impossible. The rosary is a practical and beautiful way to reverse that problem, to begin quieting our minds and our passions.

Some people dismiss the rosary as too simple, a prayer for

blue-haired church ladies. Though it's true that the rosary is a humble prayer, this is by no means a defect. Consider the humble offering of the young boy who volunteered five barley loaves to our Lord (John 6:9). That too was a simple offering, but its result was magnificent! In the same way, when we offer the five decades of the rosary through the hands of our Blessed Mother to Jesus, what can he not do?

The famous words of a bishop, Hugh Doyle, are appropriate here: "No one can live continually in sin and continue to say the rosary: Either they will give up sin or they will give up the rosary."

Scripture

The word of God is "living and active, sharper than any two-edged sword" (Heb. 4:12). Memorizing Scripture verses that pertain to purity can be of great help in moments of temptation. You'll find more than twenty such verses in the appendix of this book. Take time to meditate on them. There is power in the word of God. The Bible puts it plainly: "How can a young man keep his way pure? By guarding it according to thy word" (Ps. 119:9).

Fasting

You could say that prayer without fasting is like boxing with one hand tied behind your back, and that fasting without prayer is, well, dieting. To achieve purity, both are needed. "If you are able to fast," writes St. Francis de Sales, "you will do well to observe some days beyond what are ordered by the Church, for besides the ordinary effect of fasting in raising the mind, subduing the flesh, confirming goodness, and obtaining a heavenly reward, it is also a great matter to be able to control greediness, and to keep the sensual appetites and the whole body subject to the law of the Spirit."

A lack of self-mastery often leads to sexual sin. Fasting from legitimate pleasures, even small ones, builds up that virtue within us. When I get a plate of hot fries, I may choose to deny myself salt. When I pour myself a cup of coffee, I may choose to deny myself cream or sugar. The regular habit of denying ourselves good things gives us the inner strength to avoid bad ones. Put it this way: If we can't say no to a cookie or another slice of pizza, how will we ever say no to the temptation to look at pornography?

Here are two prayers for use in moments of temptation, found in Christopher West's excellent book, *Good News About Sex & Marriage*.

A Prayer for Purity of Heart

Lord, you have created me in your image and likeness as a man (woman). Help me to accept and receive my sexuality as a gift from you.

You have inscribed in my very being, in my sexuality, the call to love as you love, in sincere self-giving, and you have made the "one flesh" union of man and woman in marriage a sign of your own life and love in this world.

Grant me the grace always to resist the many lies that continually assail the truth and meaning of this great gift of sexuality.

Grant me purity of heart so that I might see the image of your glory in the beauty of others, and one day see you face to face.

Amen.

A Prayer in a Moment of Temptation to Lust

This is a woman (man) made in the image and likeness of God, never to be looked upon as an object for my gratification. Lord Jesus, grant me the grace to see the image of your glory in the beauty of this woman (man), and order my sexual desires towards the truth of love.

I renounce any tendency within me to use others for my own pleasure, and I unite my sufferings with yours on the cross.

Amen.

2. Become Accountable

Accountability means allowing another person to remind you of who you are and who you desire to be. It means being transparent with a trusted friend or mentor about your struggles so that he can offer encouragement and support. It's an ongoing reminder that no sin is private, that even our hidden choices can have disastrous consequences.

I have never met anyone who was able to break free from porn without accountability. No recovering porn user can be an island! We need each other. If you're Catholic, one obvious and necessary way to be accountable is to find a good confessor and stick with him. Don't "priest hop" because you're ashamed of confessing the sin again so soon. The priest is not there to judge you but to love you. Confessing to the same priest will be an opportunity to humble yourself while honestly facing the severity of your problem.

One very practical—and in my opinion essential—tool for *online accountability* is accountability software. Covenant Eyes (www.covenanteyes.com) is one of many on the market. Instead of just blocking certain websites (although it has that function also), it monitors all the sites that you visit and then sends a report to your accountability partner (it even monitors the websites behind the advertisements on the site you're visiting). Online accountability changes your Web-surfing mentality: Rather than wondering how you could get around a filter to visit some forbidden-fruit website, you will know that you *could* visit the website but that you will be held accountable for it.

When you think about it, isn't this how the heavenly Father acts toward us? He *could* "block" us from turning our backs on him and from the pain our sins bring, but he does not. Rather he teaches us right from wrong, and implores us to do what's right (while giving us the grace necessary to do it). He does not censor our every thought and action, because he desires us be responsible moral agents, sons and daughters who freely choose what is good.

Covenant Eyes seems to have figured out all the loopholes porn users will think of ahead of time. For example, if you delete your account, view porn, and then reinstall your account, your accountability partner will be notified. If the temptation to view porn at any moment threatens to overwhelm you, there is also a "panic button" you can click. Your Internet access will be disabled; the only way to get it back is to contact Covenant Eyes.

3. Counseling

Sometimes the struggle for purity requires professional help, and there are plenty of good Christian counselors who are willing and waiting to give it. Sometimes people—men especially—think that admitting they need counseling is something to be ashamed about. It is not. What *would* be shameful is realizing at the end of your life how much you and your loved ones suffered because you were too proud to seek healing.

How do you know if you may need counseling? Here are five questions to ask yourself. Answering yes to any of them could mean that you would benefit from professional counseling.

1. Do you have a preoccupation with pornography?
2. Have you made repeated unsuccessful attempts to control or stop viewing pornography?
3. Do you use pornography as a reward for hard work and/or a way to escape problems or negative emotions?
4. Are you risking the loss of a significant relationship, job, or educational or career opportunity because of the use of pornography?
5. Have you been thinking that you might need counseling because of your pornography use?

For more information, visit Integrity Restored (www.integrityrestored.com), run by clinical psychotherapist Peter Kleponis. Dr. Kleponis is a Catholic who specializes in helping those struggling to be free of pornography.

4. Educate Yourself

In the battle against pornography, it's important that we feed not only our souls but our minds. Educating yourself on the destructive nature of pornography will help convince you to break free from it. Here's what the *Catechism* has to say about it:

> Pornography consists in removing real or simulated sexual acts from the intimacy of the partners, in order to display them deliberately to third parties. It offends against chastity because it perverts the conjugal act, the intimate giving of spouses to each other. It does grave injury to the dignity of its participants (actors, vendors, the public), since each one becomes an object of base pleasure and illicit profit for others. It immerses all who are involved in the illusion of a fantasy world. It is a grave offense. Civil authorities should prevent the production and distribution of pornographic materials. (2354)

Here are some resources that will help you unpack why pornography is so harmful and destructive.

Books

Wired For Intimacy: How Pornography Hijacks the Male Brain by William M. Struthers. Dr. Struthers, a neuroscientist and researcher, explains in fascinating detail the devastating neurological effects of porn use and how they can be reversed.

The Pornography Epidemic by Peter C. Kleponis. Dr. Kleponis offers a Catholic approach to fighting porn both in our personal lives and in our culture.

The Final Freedom: Pioneering Sexual Addiction Recovery by Douglas Weiss. Clinical psychologist Weiss gives hope for recovery to those suffering from sex addiction.

The Porn Trap: The Essential Guide to Overcoming Problems Caused by Pornography by Wendy and Larry Maltz. In this book, sex and relationship therapists provide a comprehensive program for understanding and healing porn addiction and other serious consequences of porn use from a secular perspective.

Websites

www.theporneffect.com is dedicated to exposing the harmful effects of pornography.

www.beggarsdaughter.com provides helpful tools, advice, and support to women struggling with sexual sin such as pornography and masturbation.

www.chastity.com is Catholic Answers' online resource for promoting the virtue of chastity.

Articles

"Slave Master: How Pornography Drugs and Changes Your Brain" by Donald L. Hilton Jr. Neurosurgeon Hilton explains the addictive effects pornography has on the human brain. http://www.salvomag.com/new/articles/salvo13/13hilton.php

"Parenting the Porn Generation" by Matt Fradd. In this article I explain the grim reality that confronts our children today and offer practical tips about how to parent them wisely regarding the Internet. http://mattfradd.com/2012/10/22/parenting-the-porn-generation/

"Five Myths About Porn" by April Garris. Former porn actress Garris exposes five myths that are commonly believed about the porn industry. http://mattfradd.com/2012/07/18/5-myths-about-porn/

Audio Products

Taking Down Goliath by Matt Fradd. In this audio presentation I share my own story of recovery and suggest five strategies (more detailed than the ones presented here) to get porn out of your life.

The Ugly Truth: Two Former Insiders Expose the Reality Behind the Porn Industry. In this audio presentation I conduct two interviews, the first with a former porn actress and the second with a former Playboy producer. *The Ugly Truth* is a difficult but edifying listen and a sobering rebuttal to porn's lies.

Pure of Heart: Breaking Free from Porn by Jason Evert. This five-disc CD set (also available in MP3 format) provides ten tips to help men conquer their daily temptations to lust, with special emphasis on breaking free from pornography.

5. Patient Perseverance

Finally, be patient with yourself. Remember that the wounds you have received didn't come about overnight, and the healing won't take place overnight, either. It takes time, perseverance, and determination.

"Have patience with all things," urges St. Francis de Sales, "but chiefly have patience with yourself. Do not lose courage in considering your own imperfections but instantly set about remedying them—every day begin the task anew."

Several years ago, as I stood in line for the sacrament of confession, about to confess for the umpteenth time a sin I couldn't seem to quit, I began to fear that God's mercy was running out. I didn't doubt that God would pardon a person who turned to him after a life of the most heinous sins imaginable. What I did doubt was that he would continue to forgive *me*. How many times had I said, "I will never do this again," only to return to that sin like a dog to its vomit" (2 Pet. 2:22)?

At that moment—by God's grace no doubt—I was reminded of the incident in the Gospel of Matthew when Peter approached our Lord with a question:

"Then Peter came up and said to him, 'Lord, how often shall my brother sin against me, and I forgive him? As many as seven times?' Jesus said to him, 'I do not say to you seven times, but seventy times seven'" (Matt. 18:21-22).

Now, what our Lord did *not* mean was that Peter was to forgive his brother 490 times and then no more. No, rather, "seventy times seven" signified perfection and consistency. It then occurred to me: If God's forgiveness is not like that—perfect and consistent—then Jesus was commanding Peter to act in a way that was contrary to the nature of God.

The truth is, God is infinite in all his attributes. In fearing that God's mercy was slowly evaporating, I was unintentionally making God in my image. If you have ever been tempted to doubt God's mercy as I did, or if you're tempted to do that now, please ingrain the following words from St. Claude de la Colombiere into your brain:

> "I glorify You in making known how good you are towards sinners, and that your mercy prevails over all malice, that nothing can destroy it, that no matter how many times or how shamefully we fall, or how criminally, a sinner need not be driven to despair of Your pardon. . . . It is in vain that your enemy and mine sets new traps for me every day. He will make me lose everything else before the hope that I have in your mercy."

Regardless of where you have been or what you have done, be at peace. The same God who forgave Moses the murderer, Rahab the prostitute, David the adulterer, and Peter the denier will forgive you, too. All you have to do is seek that forgiveness with a contrite heart. The only sin God can't forgive is the one you will not ask forgiveness for.

Contributors

Joe McClane spent more than twenty years desperately seeking self-satisfaction, but finding nothing but shame. At the lowest point in his life, God shined his light into the darkness of Joe's life and brought him home. Since that spring day in 2002, Joe has been on a journey of conversion and discovery of God and his one, holy, catholic, and apostolic Church. You may contact Joe through his website, joemcclane.com.

Audrey Assad stumbled into a pornography addiction at the age of fifteen and spent years in silent bondage. Eventually, she found freedom and forgiveness at the hands of a merciful God and learned firsthand the power of confessing her sins aloud to another. She is a musician and a recently baptized Catholic. You can follow Audrey on Twitter @audreyassad, or visit her website, audreyassad.com.

Dr. Peter Kleponis is a Catholic therapist who specializes in men's issues. He has become a leading authority in the diagnosis and treatment of pornography addiction for Catholic men. Dr. Kleponis developed a seven-point plan for recovery that has proven to be highly effective. You may contact Dr. Kleponis through his website, integrityrestored.com.

April Garris worked as a stripper and appeared in fifteen to twenty pornographic movies. She left the industry in 2001, but continued to struggle with substance abuse, mental illness, and severe depression. It wasn't until April came to the Lord in 2005 that she began to experience true healing and has been living in freedom ever since.

Mike and Anne are grateful for the continued healing of their marriage from Mike's pornography addiction and for the continued support and healing through counseling, support groups, the sacraments, marriage retreats, and chastity resources. They are grateful to Matt Fradd for the work he is doing to spread the message of chastity and expose the lies of pornography.

Joshua Hawkins fell into using pornography in elementary school. When he tried to start living his Catholic faith fully at sixteen, he discovered he couldn't stop the compulsive behavior. Now a married professional, Joshua still struggles. But, he has found progressive victory over lust can be his through daily accountability, fellowship, prayer, and, above all, adoration and worship of the holy Eucharist.

June grew up in a small country town in Ireland. When she left for college, she began stripping to pay off a financial debt. Through the help and encouragement of Matt and Cameron Fradd, she was able to get out of the sex industry and pay off her debt. June lives and studies in Scotland.

Jessica Harris was exposed to pornography at the age of thirteen and spent eight years silently battling an addiction to lust that ranged from chat room cyber sex to hardcore pornography. Through the grace of God, Jessica found freedom and founded Beggar's Daughter, an online ministry for women struggling with pornography. She writes and speaks, sharing her story and pointing women to the hope, freedom, love, and grace found nowhere but in Christ. You may contact her at jessica@beggarsdaughter.com, or visit her website, beggarsdaughter.com.

Mark Houck is co-founder and president of The King's Men, a lay men's ministry seeking to answer the crisis in masculinity and fight pornography. He is also founder of the Samson Healing Retreat for Men (samsonretreat.com), which aims to help men who are victims of past and present abuse in their lives. He is a husband and father of three children and lives in Quakertown, Pennsylvania. You may contact Mark through his website, thekingsmen.org.

Appendix

Here are more than forty excerpts from Sacred Scripture and the writings of the saints. I encourage you to use this section for prayer and personal reflection. You may find it helpful to meditate upon a quote a day, memorizing the quote in the morning and carrying it with you throughout the day for encouragement and guidance.

I have broken the quotes from Scripture and the writings of the saints into five categories: purity, temptation, sexual sin, mercy, and Spiritual Warfare.

Sacred Scripture

While other religious and spiritual books may contain words *about* God, the Bible is the word *of* God. As St. Paul states, "All scripture is inspired by God and profitable for teaching, for reproof, for correction, and for training in righteousness, that the man of God may be complete, equipped for every good work (2 Tim. 3:16-17). Elsewhere, Paul says that "the sword of the Spirit . . . is the word of God" (Eph. 6:17). As you battle against the temptations of the flesh, then, commit these verses to memory, bringing them to mind and repeating them, especially in moments of temptation.

Purity

Blessed are the pure in heart, for they shall see God. (Matt. 5:8)

Let no one despise your youth, but set the believers an example in speech and conduct, in love, in faith, in purity. (1 Tim. 4:12)

Finally, brethren, whatever is true, whatever is honorable, whatever is just, whatever is pure, whatever is lovely, whatever is gracious, if there is any excellence, if there is anything worthy of praise, think about these things. (Phil. 4:8)

Who shall ascend the hill of the Lord? And who shall stand in his holy place? He who has clean hands and a pure heart, who does not lift up his soul to what is false. (Ps. 24:3-4)

Temptation

But each person is tempted when he is lured and enticed by his own desire. Then desire when it has conceived gives birth to sin; and sin when it is full-grown brings forth death. (James 1:14-15)

No temptation has overtaken you that is not common to man. God is faithful, and he will not let you be tempted beyond your strength, but with the temptation will also provide the way of escape, that you may be able to endure it. (1 Cor. 10:13)

So shun youthful passions and aim at righteousness, faith, love, and peace, along with those who call upon the Lord from a pure heart. (2 Tim. 2:22)

I will not set before my eyes anything that is base. I hate the work of those who fall away; it shall not cling to me. Perverseness of heart shall be far from me; I will know nothing of evil. (Ps. 101:3-4)

In all you do, remember the end of your life, and then you will never sin. (Sir. 7:36)

Sexual Sin

But I say to you that everyone who looks at a woman lustfully has already committed adultery with her in his heart. If your right eye causes you to sin, pluck it out and throw it away; it is better that you lose one of your members than that your whole body be thrown into hell. (Matt. 5:28-29)

A man who breaks his marriage vows says to himself, "Who sees me? Darkness surrounds me, and the walls hide me, and no one sees me. Why should I fear? The Most High will not take notice of my sins." His fear is confined to the eyes of men, and he does not realize that the eyes of the Lord are ten thousand times brighter than the sun; they look upon all the ways of men, and perceive even the hidden places. (Sir. 23:18)

For this is the will of God, your sanctification: that you abstain from immorality; that each one of you know how to control his own body in holiness and honor, not in the passion of lust like heathens who do not know God; that no man transgress, and wrong his brother in this matter, because the Lord is an avenger in all these things, as we solemnly forewarned you. For God has not called us for uncleanness, but in holiness. Therefore whoever disregards this, disregards not man but God, who gives his Holy Spirit to you. (1 Thess. 4:3-8)

And if your eye causes you to sin, pluck it out; it is better for you to enter the kingdom of God with one eye than with two eyes to be thrown into hell. (Mark 9:47)

Mercy

And when Jesus heard it, he said to them, "Those who are well have no need of a physician, but those who are sick; I came not to call the righteous, but sinners." (Mark 2:17)

Have mercy on me, O God, according to your merciful love; according to your abundant mercy blot out my transgressions. Wash me thoroughly from my iniquity, and cleanse me from my sin! (Ps. 51:1-2)

For I will be merciful toward their iniquities, and I will remember their sins no more. (Heb. 8:12)

As far as the east is from the west, so far does he remove our transgressions from us. (Ps. 103:12)

Spiritual Warfare

Be sober, be watchful. Your adversary the devil prowls around like a roaring lion, seeking someone to devour. Resist him, firm in your faith, knowing that the same experience of suffering is required of your brotherhood throughout the world. (1 Pet. 5:8-9)

Finally, be strong in the Lord and in the strength of his might. Put on the whole armor of God, that you may be able to stand against the wiles of the devil. For we are not contending against flesh and blood, but against the principalities, against the powers, against the world rulers of this present darkness, against the spiritual hosts of wickedness in the heavenly places.

Therefore take the whole armor of God, that you may be able to withstand in the evil day, and having done all, to stand. Stand therefore, having fastened the belt of truth around your waist, and having put on the breastplate of righteousness, and having shod your feet with the equipment of the gospel of peace; besides all these, taking the shield of faith, with which you can quench all the flaming darts of the Evil One. And take the helmet of salvation, and the sword of the Spirit, which is the word of God. (Eph. 6:10–17)

The thief comes only to steal and kill and destroy; I came that they may have life, and have it abundantly. (John 10:10)

Do not be conformed to this world but be transformed by the renewal of your mind, that you may prove what is the will of God, what is good and acceptable and perfect. (Rom. 12:2)

How can a young man keep his way pure? By guarding it according to your word. (Ps. 119:9)

The Saints

The Church distinguishes between the "Church militant," which refers to the Christians living on earth; the "Church suffering," referring to those in purgatory; and the "Church triumphant," referring to the saints in heaven. We can greatly benefit from the writings of the men and women who once lived on the earth and now reign in heaven. Here is a list of short excerpts from our brother and sister Christians who once struggled as we do now and now reign in heaven as we one day hope to.

Purity

Many live like angels in the middle of the world. You, . . . why not you?
—St. Josemaria Escriva

Only the chaste man and the chaste woman are capable of true love.
—Bl. Pope John Paul II

Purity prepares the soul for love, and love confirms the soul in purity.
—Bl. Cardinal John Henry Newman

To be pure, to remain pure, can only come at a price, the price of knowing God and loving him enough to do his will. He will always give us the strength we need to keep purity as something as beautiful for him.
—Bl. Mother Teresa

Deep within yourself, listen to your conscience, which calls you to be pure . . . a home is not warmed by the fire of pleasure, which burns quickly like a pile of withered grass. Passing encounters are only a caricature of love; they injure hearts and mock God's plan.
—Bl. Pope John Paul II

Temptation

To defend his purity, St. Francis of Assisi rolled in the snow, St. Benedict threw himself into a thorn bush, St. Bernard plunged into an icy pond. . . . You . . . what have you done?
—St. Josemaria Escriva

Filthy talk makes us feel comfortable with filthy action. But the one who knows how to control the tongue is prepared to resist the attacks of lust.
—St. Clement

Temptation is necessary to make us realize that we are nothing in ourselves.
—St. Josemaria Escriva

In temptations against chastity, the spiritual masters advise us, not so much to contend with the bad thought, as to turn the mind to some spiritual, or, at least, indifferent object. It is useful to combat other bad thoughts face to face, but not thoughts of impurity. —St. Alphonsus Liguori

He said not, "Thou shall not be tempted, thou shall not be tried, thou shall not suffer," but he did say, "Thou shall not be overcome." —Julian of Norwich

Sexual Sin

Whoever bids other folks to do right, but gives an evil example by acting the opposite way, is like a foolish weaver who weaves quickly with one hand and unravels the cloth just as quickly with the other. —St. Thomas More

Don't say, "That's the way I am—it's my character." It's your lack of character. Esto vir!—Be a man!

—St. Josemaria Escriva

When you have sought the company of a sensual satisfaction, what loneliness afterward! —St. Josemaria Escriva

Mercy

Have patience with all things, but chiefly have patience with yourself. Do not lose courage in considering your own imperfections but instantly set about remedying them—every day begin the task anew. —St. Francis de Sales

Confession heals, confession justifies, confession grants pardon of sin. All hope consists in confession. In confession there is a chance for mercy. Believe it firmly. Do not doubt, do not hesitate, never

despair of the mercy of God. Hope and have confidence in confession. —St. Isidore of Seville

God, at the moment of absolution, throws our sins over his shoulder. He forgets them; he annihilates them; they shall never reappear. —St. John Vianney

My mercy is greater without any comparison than all the sins creatures can commit. Therefore it greatly displeases me that they should consider their sins to be greater.

—Catherine of Sienna,
recording the words of Jesus in a private revelation

I glorify you in making known how good you are towards sinners, and that your mercy prevails over all malice, that nothing can destroy it, that no matter how many times or how shamefully we fall, or how criminally, a sinner need not be driven to despair of your pardon. . . . It is in vain that your enemy and mine sets new traps for me every day. He will make me lose everything else before the hope that I have in your mercy.
—St. Claude de la Colombiere

The good Lord is more eager to pardon a repentant sinner than a mother [is] to rescue her child from the fire.

—St. John Vianney

Spiritual Warfare

We need to be especially alert to the evil subtlety of Satan. His one desire is to keep people from having a mind and heart disposed to their Lord and God. . . . He wants to extinguish the light of the human heart, and so he moves in by means of worldly busyness and worry. —St. Francis of Assisi

The Spirit of God is a spirit of peace. Even in the most serious faults he makes us feel a sorrow that is tranquil, humble, and confident. This is precisely because of his mercy. The spirit of the devil, instead, excites, exasperates, and makes us feel, in that very sorrow, anger against ourselves. We should, on the contrary, be charitable with ourselves first and foremost. Therefore if any thought agitates you, this agitation never comes from God, who gives you peace, being the spirit of peace, but from the devil.

—St. Pio of Pietrelcina

The devil only tempts those souls that wish to abandon sin and those that are in a state of grace. The others belong to him; he has no need to tempt them.

—St. John Vianney

From long experience I have learned that there is nothing like holy water to put devils to flight and prevent them from coming back again. They also flee from the Cross, but return; so holy water must have great virtue.

—St. Teresa of Avila

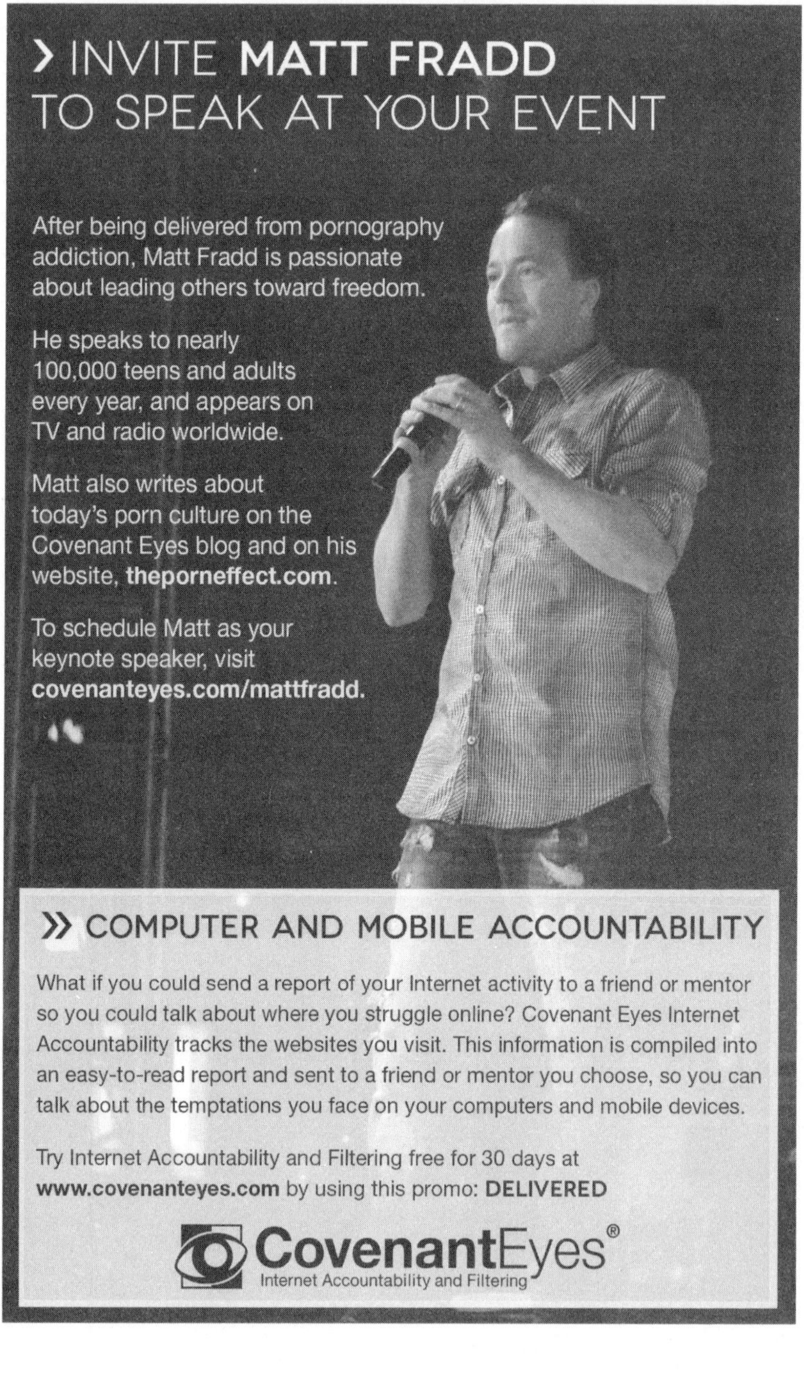

› INVITE **MATT FRADD** TO SPEAK AT YOUR EVENT

After being delivered from pornography addiction, Matt Fradd is passionate about leading others toward freedom.

He speaks to nearly 100,000 teens and adults every year, and appears on TV and radio worldwide.

Matt also writes about today's porn culture on the Covenant Eyes blog and on his website, **theporneffect.com**.

To schedule Matt as your keynote speaker, visit **covenanteyes.com/mattfradd.**

» COMPUTER AND MOBILE ACCOUNTABILITY

What if you could send a report of your Internet activity to a friend or mentor so you could talk about where you struggle online? Covenant Eyes Internet Accountability tracks the websites you visit. This information is compiled into an easy-to-read report and sent to a friend or mentor you choose, so you can talk about the temptations you face on your computers and mobile devices.

Try Internet Accountability and Filtering free for 30 days at **www.covenanteyes.com** by using this promo: **DELIVERED**